顽皮小丫的**英语**征服记

对答如流

顽皮小丫的

美国见闻

主审：杨　阳

编著：芝麻门外语编辑部

大连理工大学出版社

DALIAN UNIVERSITY OF TECHNOLOGY PRESS

图书在版编目（CIP）数据

对答如流：顽皮小丫的美国见闻 / 芝麻门外语编辑
部编著 . — 大连：大连理工大学出版社，2014.9
（顽皮小丫的英语征服记）
ISBN 978-7-5611-9344-0

Ⅰ.①对… Ⅱ.①芝… Ⅲ.①英语－口语 Ⅳ.
① H319.9

中国版本图书馆 CIP 数据核字 (2014) 第 162190 号

大连理工大学出版社出版
地址：大连市软件园路 80 号　　邮政编码：116023
发行：0411-84708842 邮购：0411-84703636 传真：0411-84701466
E-mail:dutp@dutp.cn　　URL: http://www.dutp.cn
大连永盛印业有限公司印刷　　大连理工大学出版社发行

幅面尺寸：140mm×203mm
字数：265 千字
2014 年 9 月第 1 版

印张：10.625
印数：1~4000
2014 年 9 月第 1 次印刷

责任编辑：钟　宇
装帧设计：对岸书影

责任校对：郭欣田
插画：胡楠 夏仟仟

ISBN 978-7-5611-9344-0

定价：32.00 元

如果您的英语底子薄，或者您干脆就是"忘光一族"，甚至是"英语零起点"……

如果您认为在中国学英语根本学不地道，学到的将会是生涩的"哑巴英语"……

如果您正期待着一场异国恋情，或者您心中的TA是个"老外"……

如果您准备到欧美留学或者自助旅游，又或者您将被派到欧美工作、出差……

那么，请您选择这套《顽皮小丫的英语征服记》系列丛书，它将绝对不会让您后悔！

本套丛书按照英语学习的规律和难易程度，共分为《32天闯关——顽皮小丫的英语入门》《对答如流——顽皮小丫的美国见闻》和《职场闯关——顽皮小丫的职场成长》三本。该系列丛书以乐观开朗的中国女孩——小丫为主人公，以在她身边发生的事情为故事主线。从小丫零起点学习英语，到赴美游学的亲身经历，再到美国职场的辛苦打拼，最后她终于能够轻松驾驭英语并深度了解美国文化。故事中，有在美国生活的见闻，有难得的友情，也有中西方文化的冲突，但这些都是小丫英语语言积

累的源泉。只要您跟随着小丫的脚步，您就会像她一样，最后能够熟练应用英语。学英语，真的就是这么简单！

本书为《对答如流——顽皮小丫的美国见闻》，是为初次去美国学习或者旅游的人士精心编写的。从这一刻起，我们的主人公小丫已经可以独自踏上美国之旅了。

全书共分为32课，从小丫步入肯尼迪机场开始，到日后逐渐融入到学校的生活，期间有师生相处的点点滴滴，有朋友之间的谈天说地，内容包括了生活所需的衣食住行。本书从读者的需求出发，场景不同，其表达方式也不同，既有语言的学习，也有知识的介绍。

希望本书以最贴切的生活场景、通俗易懂的语言表达方式，帮助读者了解美国，度过愉快的异国之旅。

本书在编写过程中，得到了杨阳老师的细心指导，同时，编委会的成员盛丹丹、马凤萍、肖红岩、王英辉、王雪峰老师也参与到本书的编写工作中，在此，一并对以上老师表示由衷的感谢。

最后，期待这套汇集众多旅居美国的学者智慧的、历时三年的"呕心之作"能够为您成功地敲开英语学习的大门！期待这次"狠下心来学英语"是您最后的、最成功的决心！

编　者

2014年9月

目 录

顽皮小丫的 英语征服记

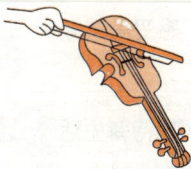

小丫
Ya

北京女孩。是热情、活泼、执着的浪漫主义者。对美国有着浓厚的兴趣，19岁就只身背上行囊，踏上向往已久的国度——美国。

Nancy
南希

美国女孩。小丫在国内的短期英语家教，北京语言大学中文专业的交换生，中文很好。教会了小丫一些简单的英语语法和一些最基本的对话，两人因此也成为了好朋友。

汤姆 TOM

南希的同学。纽约大学数学系的学生，是个充满阳光和朝气的美国大男孩，对中国有着浓厚的兴趣。一直帮助小丫，并被这位独立的中国女孩深深地打动了。

杰瑞 Jerry

汤姆的室友。纽约大学计算机科学系的高材生。心地善良，思维敏捷，但常常把科技术语挂在嘴边，给人科学狂人的印象。

第1课

机场初相见：汤姆来接机

情景介绍：清晨，在纽约肯尼迪机场，汤姆翘首企盼了一个小时，才看见小丫面带笑容地推着行李车走出来……

会话1

Tom: Good morning, Ya!

Ya: Good morning, Tom!

Tom: Nice to meet you in person!

Ya: Nice to meet you too. Sorry to keep you waiting. I had some trouble with my luggage.

Tom: Was it serious? You've got all your stuff?

Ya: It's nothing serious. I've got all my luggage now.

Tom: That's good. How was your flight?

Ya: The flight was excellent! I've already experienced some America with American Airways.

Tom: Well, welcome to America!

Ya: Thank you and America! How do we get to the city?

Tom: Let's take the airport shuttle. It's connected with the metro line.

Ya: Sounds good. I'll follow you.

汤姆:	小丫，早上好！
小丫:	汤姆，早上好！
汤姆:	终于见到你的庐山真面目了！
小丫:	见到你我也很高兴。对不起让你久等了，我的行李出了点问题。
汤姆:	严重吗？行李都拿到了？
小丫:	没什么大问题，现在行李都拿到了。
汤姆:	那就好。旅途如何？
小丫:	真棒！美国航空已经让我有了美国初体验。
汤姆:	好啊，欢迎来到美国！
小丫:	谢谢你，也谢谢美国！我们怎么去市内啊？
汤姆:	我们坐机场大巴，大巴线路是和地铁对接的。
小丫:	听起来不错。我跟着你走。

会话2

Ya: Thank you for coming to the airport! You are the first person I've known in the US.

Tom: You are welcome. I'm sure you will have many other friends in the near future.

Ya: How did you recognize me?

Tom: Remember? We talked on Skype before you came here.

Ya: You've got sharp eyes.

Tom: I'll take this as a compliment. By the way, my roommate Jerry and his girlfriend Jessica are fascinated with China. They will be thrilled to see you.

Ya: Tom and Jerry! You are like the cartoons.

Tom: You are not the first one to say so. We are just good friends.

Ya: Don't take it the wrong way. It was a joke.

Tom: Don't worry. American people like joking.

Ya: What a relief!

> **小丫：** 谢谢你来机场接我！你是我在美国认识的第一个人呢。
>
> **汤姆：** 别客气。我相信不久你就会有很多其他朋友的。
>
> **小丫：** 你怎么认出我来的?
>
> **汤姆：** 不记得了？你来美国前我们在网络电话上聊过天。
>
> **小丫：** 你眼力真不错。

汤姆：	我就当作你在表扬我吧。对了，我的室友杰瑞和他女朋友杰西卡对中国很着迷。他们见到你一定高兴死了。
小丫：	汤姆和杰瑞！你们俩像《猫和老鼠》的动画片。
汤姆：	你已经不是第一个这么说的了。我们只是好朋友而已。
小丫：	你别误会，我是开玩笑的。
汤姆：	别担心。美国人喜欢开玩笑。
小丫：	这我就放心了！

必备词汇

airport shuttle ['ʃʌtl] n.

机场巴士，机场大巴，机场班车

注 shuttle本意为织机的梭子，和airport合用，解释为机场巴士。另外，shuttle又意航天飞机和羽毛球等。

airport
['ɛəpɔ:t] n.

机场，航空港

airways
['ɛəweiz] n.

航空公司

注 airway单数意为空中航线，复数意为航空公司。

cartoons
[ka:'tu:nz] n.

卡通片，动画片

注 cartoon也是动画片、卡通片的意思。因为《猫和老鼠》是系列动画片，所以以复数形式出现。

compliment
['kɔmplimənt] n.

恭维，称赞，赞扬

注意区分complement n.补充，不足，补语，二者在拼写上有细微差别。

excellent
['eksələnt] adj.

极佳的，杰出的，卓越的

experience
[ik'spiəriəns] n.

体验，经验

注 experience意为体验、经验时是不可数名词，但意为某人的经历时是可数名词，比如The writer shared his experiences in Africa with us. 这位作家和我们分享了他的非洲经历。另外，experience也有动词词性，意为"体验，经验，经历"。

fascinated
['fæsineitid] adj.

着迷的，被深深吸引的

注 fascinated基于动词fascinate v. 强烈地吸引，迷住。注意区分fascinating adj. 吸引人的，令人着迷的。

例如 Chinese culture is really fascinating. 中国文化的确令人着迷。

flight
[flait] n.

飞行，航程，航班，班机

luggage
['lʌgidʒ] n.

行李，皮箱，箱包

注 同义词为baggage n.

metro
['metrəu] n.

地铁

注 同义词为subway n.

relief
[ri'li:f] n.

轻松，解除，安慰

注 sigh of relief 轻松地叹气，长舒一口气

thrilled
[θrild] adj.

非常兴奋的，极为激动的

注 区分thrilling adj. 令人兴奋的，震撼人心的，例如 The most thrilling part was the arrival of Santa Claus. 最令人兴奋的莫过于圣诞老人的出现了。

地道美语

1 **Don't take it the wrong way.** 别误会。如果无心说了可能令 / 让对方误解的话，要赶紧解释，以免造成更大的误会。比如：

A: Don't take it the wrong way. I wasn't meaning to tease you.

B: Don't worry. I know what you mean.

　　A: 别误会。我没想嘲笑你。
　　B: 别担心，我明白你的意思。

2 **It's nothing serious.** 没什么大不了的事，没什么大毛病。对于不严重的问题说一句"没什么大不了的"，免得对方担心。比如：

A: You didn't come to school yesterday. Are you all right?

B: I had some headache, but it's nothing serious.

　　A: 你昨天没来学校，不要紧吧？
　　B: 我有些头疼，不过没什么大毛病。

3 **Sounds good.** 听起来不错。如果伙伴们有好主意，就不要吝惜你的赞许哦。比如：

A: How about going to the cinema this Sunday?

B: Sounds good. I'd like to see a movie.

　　A: 这周日去电影院怎么样？
　　B: 听起来不错。我想看场电影呢。

④ Take it as a compliment. 把……当作赞美。是一种幽默的表达方法，如果对方语气里有赞许的意味，那么就欣然接受吧！比如：

A: You always have good ideas which other people can't come up with.

B: I'll take it as a compliment. I like original things.

A: 你总是有别人想不到的好主意。

B: 我就把你的话当作赞美吧。我喜欢新颖的事物。

⑤ What a relief! 那就放心了！相信我们都有如释重负的时刻，这种心情要如何地道地表达出来呢？比如：

A: I thought I couldn't pass the exam. I made it!

B: Congratulations! What a relief!

A: 我还以为考试过不了呢。我竟然过了！

B: 恭喜你！这下放心了！

表达方式百宝箱

不熟悉的朋友初次见面免不了要互相问候。在本课中小丫和汤姆使用了一些英语中常见的问候语，现在我们一起总结一下吧！

Good afternoon! 下午好！

Good evening! 晚上好！

Good morning! 早上好！

Nice to meet/ see you. 认识/见到你很高兴。

Sorry to keep you waiting. 抱歉让你久等了。

Thank you for coming to the airport! 谢谢你来机场接我。

Welcome to America! 欢迎来到美国！

小丫 带你走遍美国

大苹果市——美国纽约市的别称

根据纽约历史学会（New York Historical Society）资料显示，"大苹果"这个别称可以追溯至1921年《纽约晨递报》（The New York Morning Telegraph）的一位作者John J. Fitz Gerald。约翰在报上主要是撰写赛马专栏的，他在赛马场跟来自于纽奥良的黑人马夫聊天时，得知他们对于有机会来到纽约兴奋不已，在他们眼中，纽约是个遍地黄金且充满机会的地方，就以"大苹果（Big Apple）"作为形容，意思是既好看又好吃，人人都想咬上一口。自此之后，"大苹果市"的说法广为流传，尤其流行于纽约哈林区的黑人爵士乐表演者之间。到了20世纪70年代，"大苹果"之名已逐渐被世人淡忘，但当时的旅游局为了以新颖的方式宣传纽约市，又因为苹果代表健康，所以决定以苹果作为标志。"大苹果"现已被公认为纽约市的别称，这也象征纽约健康有活力、多元化的特征。我们的小丫来到纽约正是为了抓住机遇，实现自己的梦想。

第2课

学校注册：新学期要开始了

情景介绍： 经过一天的休息，还在时差影响中的小丫上午来到学校，按照校园地图的指示找到了注册办公室。昏昏欲睡的感觉完全被对新学校和新生活的向往冲淡了。

会话1

Ya: Good morning, madam. My name is Ya. I am here to register for the new semester.

Office Lady: Good morning. Sure, come on in and have a seat.

Ya: Thank you.

Office Lady: Your name is Ya Jiang, right? May I have your passport and the admission letter, please?

Ya: Of course. Here they are.

Office Lady: Right. Let me check. (After a few minutes…) I'm going to put your information in the system and then make a photocopy of these documents. Wait a second.

Ya: No problem. Take your time.

Office Lady: All right. You are now officially registered in New York University as an undergraduate student. Welcome and congratulations! Here is your passport and documents. This is your student card.

Ya: Thank you again. The student card looks different from the one I had in China.

Office Lady: Oh, really? I assume you will find other pleasant differences during your stay in the United States. Have a nice day, Ya.

Ya: You, too.

小丫： 老师，早上好。我是小丫，我来办理新学期注册的相关事宜。

办公室老师： 早上好。好的，进来吧，请坐。

小丫： 谢谢。

办公室老师： 你的名字是蒋小丫，对吧？我可以看一下你的护照和录取通知书吗？

小丫： 当然可以了。给您。

办公室老师： 好的。我来核实一下。（几分钟以后……）我现在把你的信息输入到系统中，然后复印一下你的证件和材料。请稍等。

小丫： 没问题，不急。

办公室老师： 好了。现在你已经正式注册为纽约大学的本科新生。欢迎你加入我们，并祝贺你！请收好你的护照和材料。这是你的学生证。

小丫： 再次谢谢您。这个学生证和我以前在中国的不一样。

办公室老师： 噢，真的吗？我想你在美国这段时间还会发现其他和中国不一样的地方。祝你今天愉快，小丫。

小丫： 也祝您愉快。

会话2

Office Lady: Welcome on board, Ya. Are you up for a campus tour?

Ya: A campus tour? That's great. I'd love it!

Office Lady: But before we start, I'm going to ask you a few questions, which will help us to get a better knowledge of your condition and see if we can help you somehow.

Ya:	It's very nice of you and our university.
Office Lady:	Where are you staying right now?
Ya:	I'm staying in a youth hostel nearby, but I'd like to find a home-stay family.
Office Lady:	This is a brilliant idea. It will not only help you with your English, and also give you a comprehensive picture of American culture, which is really important if you intend to stay long in the U.S..
Ya:	Indeed, this is exactly what I thought.
Office Lady:	Since you already know what you want, we can begin with the files I have. You know, we need to confirm our students are staying in the right place, with the right people.
Ya:	I'm thinking to stay with a retired couple, whose children are living in other cities.
Office Lady:	I see. What's your budget for the rent?

Ya: I guess between 600 and 800 dollars, otherwise it will be too much for me.

Office Lady: Exactly. Let's make some appointments.

Ya: Perfect!

办公室老师： 欢迎你加入我们，小丫！你有兴趣参观校园吗？

小丫： 参观校园？太好了！我喜欢这个主意！

办公室老师： 但是在我们出发之前，我要问你一些问题，便于我们对你的情况有更好的了解，看看能否在哪些方面给你一些帮助。

小丫： 您和校方真是太好了。

办公室老师： 你现在住在哪儿？

小丫： 我现在住在附近的青年旅社，但是我想找一个寄宿家庭。

办公室老师： 这是个非常好的想法。寄宿家庭不仅可以帮助你提高英语水平，还会让你对美国文化有更完整的了解。如果你要长期住在美国的话，这一点是很重要的。

小丫： 确实，这也正是我所想的。

办公室老师： 既然你心里已经有了目标，我们可以从我手头的资料开始。你要知道，校方需要确保我们的学生住在安全的地方，跟积极的人群交往。

小丫： 我想和一对退休夫妇一起住，最好他们的孩子都住在外地。

办公室老师： 我知道了。那你的预算大概是多少呢？

小丫： 我觉得600到800美元之间，不然就太贵了。

办公室老师： 完全理解。让我们先预约几个吧。

小丫： 好极了！

必备词汇

admission letter
[əd'miʃnə] n.

录取信，录取通知书
admission n. 进入许可，入场券，门票。
例如 Students have free admission to all school facilities. 学生可以免费使用学校的各项设施。

assume
[ə'sju:m] v.

认为，以为，假定
例如 The lawyer assumes she is innocent. 这位律师认为她是无辜的。

comprehensive
[kɔmpri'hensiv] adj.

全面的，综合的
例如 Globalization is indeed comprehensive transformation of the society. 全球化确实是一种全面的社会变迁。

confirm
[kən'fə:m] v.

确认，确保
例如 Please confirm your order before any payment. 请在付款前确认您的订单。

home-stay n.

寄宿家庭。这是欧美留学生活中比较受欢迎的居住方式，就是和当地居民一起居住。
例如 The university helps new students to arrange their accomodation in home-stay. 大学帮助新生安排住在当地居民家中。

intend
[in'tend] v.

准备，计划，打算

例如 We intend to spend the night in the countryside. 我们打算在乡下住一晚。

officially
[ə'fiʃəli] adv.

正式地

例如 The statement has been officially signed by both parties. 此项声明已由双方正式签署。

photocopy
['fəutəˌkɔpi] n.

影印，复印；v. 影印，复印

例如 Please photocopy all your original documents. 请复印所有文件的原件。

register
['redʒistə] v.

登记，注册

例如 Mr. Smith went to the city hall to register the birth of his son. 史密斯先生去市政厅为他儿子做出生登记。同时register也是名词，**例如** There is no register of his death. 没有关于他的死亡记录。

retire
[ri'taiə] v.

退休

例如 The average age for American people to retire is 65. 美国人的平均退休年龄是65岁。

semester
[si'mestə] n.

学期，半学年

term n. 是同义词，但semester是偏美式的用法。**例如** When does the new semester begin? 新学期什么时候开始？

undergraduate
[ˌʌndəˈgrædjuət] n.

大学生，本科生

graduate　n. 大学毕业生。**例如** My sister is an undergraduate student at Yale University, but I am a graduate. 我妹妹是耶鲁大学的本科生，但我已经毕业了。

youth hostel
[ˈhɔstəl] n.

青年旅社，青年旅馆

hostel　n. 旅馆，旅社，规模比hotel（n. 宾馆，饭店，酒店）要小。

地道美语

① Come on in. 请进。／快进来吧。意思和Come in相同，但是是美国人习惯的口语表达方法。例如，有新邻居搬到你的小区，你带着小礼物去他家拜访。

You: Hi, I heard you just moved in this street two days ago. Here is a little house-warming present.

New neighbor: It's so nice of you. Come on in!

你： 我听说你们两天前才搬到这条街上。这是一份小礼物，欢迎你们。

新邻居： 你真是太客气了。快请进！

② Wait a second. 请稍等。这里的second并不是真正的一秒钟，是一种夸张的说法，但表明时间很短，让对方不必担心。而Take your time 意为"不着急"，正是完美的回答方式。也是为了让对方安心。比如在打电话时出现了下面的小状况：

A: Hold a second. My mom is talking to me.
B: No problem. Take your time.

A: 稍等一下。我妈妈在跟我说话。
B: 没问题，不着急。

③ Have a nice day! 祝你有美好的一天。／祝你今天愉快。这种用法可以推广到 Have a nice evening, Have a nice weekend, Have a nice trip, 分别意为：晚上愉快。／周末愉快。／旅途愉快。是给对方礼貌的祝福。在日常对话中经常用到。例如：

A: I'm going to Spain for a holiday!
B: Cool. Have a nice holiday.

A: 我要去西班牙度假。
B: 太酷了。度假愉快。

④ Indeed, Exactly、确实、千真万确。是对说话人的肯定，所以在和美国人聊天的时候就别 yes、yes 地说个没完啦。例如：

A: The housing price in China is incredibly high.
B: Indeed. It's too hard for young people to afford a house.
A: Exactly. That's what I mean.

A: 中国的房价太高了。
B: 确实是这样。年轻人几乎负担不起一栋房子。
A: 千真万确。我正是这个意思。

⑤ Are you up for a campus tour? 你有兴趣参观校园吗？ be up for 意为"打算，考虑，有兴趣"，是口语化的表达方式。campus tour 意为参观校园，因此引申 bus tour 意为坐巴士观光。比如：

A: Have you tried the bus tour around New York? It's amazing!

B: Really? I'm going to try it!

A: 你试过坐巴士参观纽约了吗？酷毙了！

B: 真的吗？我要试一试！

6 I'd love it! 太好了！／我喜欢这个主意！如果对方有好的提议，就要马上表达自己的赞同和喜悦之情哦。例如：

A: I heard there is a new cinema in town. Why don't we check it out this weekend?

B: I'd love it!

A: 我听说镇上新开了一家影院。这周末我们去试一试，怎么样？

B: 太好了！

7 What's your budget for the rent? 你对房租的预算是多少？budget n. 预算，预算费；经费。消费总是要量力而行，因此budget对我们的意义非比寻常。例如：

A: She tries to keep her monthly budget below $500.

B: It's quite hard if she needs to pay the rent.

A: 她试图把每月的开支限制在500美元以下。

B: 如果她还要交房租的话是很困难的。

表达方式百宝箱

本课中出现了在交际对话及正式场合中用到的金牌表达方式，下面我们就来总结一下吧。

Come on in./ Come in. 请进。
Have a nice day. 祝你今天愉快。
Have a nice holiday. 祝你假期愉快。
Have a nice trip. 祝你旅途愉快。
Have a nice weekend. 祝你周末愉快。
Have a seat. 请坐。
I'd love it! 我太喜欢（这个主意）了!
Take your time. 不着急。
Wait a second./ Wait a minute./ Wait a moment. 请稍等一会儿。

小丫 带你走遍 美国

Home-stay —— 寄宿家庭

　　寄宿家庭是面向留学生在国内生活的不便而产生的当地寄宿家庭。出于对未成年孩子出国的安全考虑，一般选择这类家庭，一来可以迅速熟悉当地的生活方式，二来有人照顾起居，也可以更好地提高自己的当地语言水平。一般情况下home-stay的家长都会被指定为入住学生的监护人。在中国又称home-stay住家项目。home-stay在很多西方国家，尤其是美国都很受欢迎。通常，home-stay是非常有意义的，能帮助不同国籍的人分享经验、交流文化、共享信息。但想要home-stay的留学生往往是第一次远离自己的国家和家人，缺乏必要的经验。同时互联网上的诈骗现在也越来越常见，特别是需要国际支付时，风险控制变得非常复杂。因此不管是东道方还是留学生方，都要尽量联系信誉度高的教育机构和中介。我们的主人公小丫在办公室老师的帮助下，找到了称心如意的寄宿家庭，可谓是皆大欢喜。

第3课

去银行: 可以兑换旅行支票吗?

情景介绍: 小丫出国前准备了少量的现金, 现在要交学费了, 所以小丫决定把国内旅行支票兑换成现金。阳光明媚的上午, 小丫来到了地处第三大街 (3rd Avenue) 的美国运通 (American Express) 。

会话1

Reception Desk: Good morning, Miss. May I help you?

Ya: Yes. I'd like to change a traveler's cheque.

Reception Desk: I see. Do you have a reservation?

Ya: Oh no, I don't. I didn't know a reservation would be needed.

Reception Desk: It's not always necessary, but we need to make sure our cash flow is big enough.

Ya: I hope it's not a problem.

Reception Desk: Please wait a second. I'm going to check with my colleague.

Ya: Sure. Take your time.

(After a few minutes)

Reception Desk: Miss, please follow me, I'll take you to my colleague's office.

Ya: All right. After you.

Reception Desk: You can discuss the details with my colleague.

Ya: Thank you for your help. I also need to consult about the bank account.

Reception Desk: I'm sure you will get the perfect answers.

前台: 早上好，小姐。有什么我可以帮助您的吗？

小丫: 是的，我想兑换旅行支票。

前台: 好的。您有预约吗？

小丫: 哦，没有。我不知道还需要提前预约。

前台: 也不是一定要预约，但是我们需要保证银行有足够的现金。

小丫: 我希望没问题。

前台：请稍等片刻。我去跟同事确认一下。

小丫：当然，不着急。

（几分钟后）

前台：小姐，请跟我来，我带您去同事的办公室。

小丫：好的，我跟着你。

前台：您可以跟我的同事讨论细节问题。

小丫：谢谢你的帮助。我还要咨询一些关于银行账户的问题。

前台：我保证您将得到满意的答案。

会话2

Bank clerk: Good morning, Miss. Please have a seat.

Ya: Good morning, Madam. I'd like to cash a traveler's cheque.

Bank clerk: Yes, of course. May I take a look at your traveler's cheque?

Ya: Yes, sure. Here it is.

Bank clerk: So the amount is $10,000. How much do you want to cash?

Ya: I want to cash all of it.

Bank clerk: Are you serious? I wouldn't recommend it. I'm not saying New York isn't safe, but a young girl walking around with $10,000 cash isn't very wise.

Ya: Oh…I never thought about it. You see, the semester is coming up, and there are so many things I need to pay for.

Bank clerk: I completely understand your situation. Have you considered starting a bank account in New York? You can use the card in most places here.

Ya: This is a great idea. Can I start an account right here right now?

Bank clerk: No problem, Miss. To start an account I need your ID card or passport.

Ya: Right. This is my passport, because I don't have an ID card yet.

Bank clerk: OK. You need to fill in these papers, and I'll make a copy of this in the meantime.

(After a moment)

Bank clerk: Now would you put in an eight-digital code, Miss Jiang?

Ya: Eight-digital? It's longer than the Chinese one.

Bank clerk: It's done. Here is your bank card, Miss Jiang.

Ya: Thank you so much. Have a nice day.

Bank clerk: You, too.

银行职员：早上好，小姐，请坐。

小丫：早上好，女士，我想兑换旅行支票。

银行职员：是的，我知道。我可以看一下您的旅行支票吗？

小丫：好的，当然可以，给您。

银行职员：这是一万美元的旅行支票。你想兑换多少？

小丫：我想全部兑换。

银行职员：真的吗？我不建议您这样做。我并不是在说纽约不安全，但是一位年轻女孩带着这么多的现金走在街上是不明智的行为。

小丫：哦⋯⋯我从来没考虑过。您看，新学期马上开始了，我要付很多钱。

银行职员：我完全理解您的处境。您考虑过在纽约开个银行账户吗？在这里，大部分地方您都可以刷卡付费。

小丫：这是个好主意。我可以现在就在这开个账户吗？

银行职员：没问题的，小姐。要开户的话，您需要把身份证或者护照给我。

小丫：好的，这是我的护照，因为我现在还没有身份证。

银行职员：好的。您需要填这些表格，我去把您的护照复印一份。

（过了一会儿）

银行职员：现在请您输入8位数的密码，蒋小姐。

小丫：8位数？比中国的密码长。

银行职员：好了。这是您的银行卡，蒋小姐。

小丫：非常感谢。祝您度过愉快的一天。

银行职员：您也是。

必备词汇

account
[ə'kaunt] n.

账户，户头
bank account n. 银行账户
accountant n. 会计，会计师
accounting firm n. 会计师事务所
例如 She doesn't have much money on her account at the end of the month. 月底她的账户上没有多少钱。

cash flow
[fləu] n.

现金流，现金流转
这是各类企业保证正常运转的重要条件。**例如** Our company is suffering from cash flow problem. 我们公司正深受现金流转问题的困扰。

consider
[kən'sidə] v.

考虑，打算
习惯用法是consider后面接动词的ing形式，意为考虑做某事。**例如** Have you considered learning another language? 你考虑过学一门外语吗？

consult
[kən'sʌlt] v.

商量，咨询
consultant n. 顾问，咨询者。现在比较流行的consulting firm n. 咨询公司。**例如** You should consult your parents. 你应该和父母商量一下。He works in a consulting firm as a senior consultant. 他在一家咨询公司做高级顾问。

digital
['dɪdʒɪtəl] n.

数字，数码

例如 This code consists six digitals. 这个密码包含六位数字。My brother bought a new digital camera. 我哥哥买了一部新的数码相机。

discuss
[dis'kʌs] v.

讨论，探讨

discussion n. 讨论，研究，探讨。
例如 He discussed the question with his parents. 他和父母讨论了这个问题。This problem needs further discussion. 这个问题需要进一步讨论。

ID Card

身份证

是Identification Card的缩写形式。
例如 You need to take your ID Card along. 你需要把身份证带在身上。

recommend
[ˌrekə'mend] v.

建议，参照，推荐

letter of recommendation 推荐信
例如 The professor recommended his students to be patient, for learning a language is not an exam to take, but a lifestyle to face with. 这位教授建议他的学生要有耐心，因为学习语言不是考一场试，而是去面对一种生活方式。

reservation
[ˌrezə'veɪʃən] n.

预约，预订

如果去比较受欢迎的餐厅或者宾馆，提前预订是必要的。例如 I'll arrive late, but please keep my reservation. 我会晚到一会儿，请保留我预约的房间。

traveler's cheque [tʃek]

旅行支票

cheque n. 支票。cheque book n. 支票本，支票簿。本课中出现的cash a traveler's cheque意为兑换旅行支票。

wise [waiz] adj.

智慧的，明智的

wisdom n. 智慧，才智，学识。

例如 He has made a wise decision. 他做了一个明智的决定。Wisdom is the fountain of life. 智慧是生命的源泉。

地道美语

① **After you.** 您先请。/您先。/在您之后。可以用来表现绅士风度，也可以用来表现对听话者的尊敬。例如：

Jack and Ya are going to a restaurant. At the entrance, Jack will say to Ya: After you. Ya will give a smile and be the first one to enter.

杰克和小丫正要去一家餐厅。在门口，杰克会对小丫说：你先请（女士优先）。而此时小丫的回应应该是一个微笑然后在杰克前面进入餐厅。

② **Are you serious?** 真的吗？/你是认真的吗？如果对方的话让你觉得难以置信，会自然而然表达这样的感慨。同义的表达方式还有Seriously? 更为简洁，也更为口语化。例如：

Jack: I'm considering biking to Tibet.

Ya: Seriously? That's a really long way.

杰克：我打算骑自行车去西藏。

小丫：你是认真的吗？那可是很远的路呢。

③ Here it is. 在这。/给你。再递给对方东西时以提起对方的注意，也是一种礼貌的表达方式。例如：

Airport officer: Please present your passport, Miss.

Ya: Here it is, sir.

机场警察：请出示您的护照，小姐。

小丫：给您，警官。

④ I completely understand your situation. 我完全理解你的处境。是安慰对方或者表示与对方感同身受的说法。例如：

Ya: I'm all alone in the US, so I have to stand on my own feet.

Jack: I completely understand your situation.

小丫：我在美国孤身一人，所以我必须要依靠自己。

杰克：我完全理解你的处境。

stand on one's own feet 意为"自立，自食其力，依靠自己"。例如：

In the US, young people need to stand on their own feet after they are 18.

在美国，年轻人18岁以后就要开始自立了。

⑤ I wouldn't recommend it. 我不建议这样做。是对说话人的意见表示不赞同的委婉说法。对比 I don't agree. 和 It's not a good idea. 语气更容易被对方接受，也更加正式。例如：

Ya: I'd like to join four student communities this year. It's so hard to choose, because I like them all.

Jack: I wouldn't recommend it. If you join four communities, you won't have enough time to study. You need to make a decision.

小丫：今年我想加入四个学生社团。太难选择了，因为我四个都很喜欢。

杰克：我不建议这样做。如果你加入四个学生社团，就没有时间学习了，所以你需要做出个决定。

6 In the meantime. 与此同时。与meanwhile和at the same time意思相同，但更适用于正式场合和与上司长辈的对话中。例如：

In the train accident, many people were killed, but meanwhile there were some who were unhurt.

在这次火车事故中，死了许多人，但与此同时也有一些人没有受伤。

The booming economy is bringing profit to the country, but in the meantime the pollution brought by it is also increasing.

增长的经济给国家带来利益，但与此同时随之而来的污染也在加重。

7 May I help you?/ Can I help you?/ What can I do for you? 我能帮助你吗？/我能为你做些什么？去银行、商店，服务人员会礼貌地问你需要什么帮助。例如：

Shop assistant: May I help you, sir?

Steven: Yes, please. I'm looking **for** a watch as a birthday gift for my **dau**ghter.

售货员: 我能帮助您吗, 先生?

史蒂文: 是的, 我想买一块表作为女儿的生日礼物。

⑧ Right here, right now. 就在这儿, 此时。是两个独立的词组, 可以分开使用, 也可以同时使用。例如:

The great writer Shakespeare was born **righ**t here in this house.

伟大的作家莎士比亚正是在这座房子里出生的。

Right now taking on part-time jobs in **you**r spare time is a great cash cow.

现在, 利用业余时间做点兼职是一个很好的"财源"。

cash cow 意为"财源, 摇钱树"。例如: This product has always been a cash cow for our company. 这项产品一直是我们公司的摇钱树。

表达方式百宝箱

本课中我们又学习了新的表达方式, 现在就让我们一起来总结一下吧。

After you. 您先。

Do you have a reservation? 你有预约吗?

I'd like to cash a traveler's cheque. 我想兑换旅行支票。

May I help you? 我能帮助你吗？

Thanks for your help. 谢谢你的帮助。

小丫 带你走遍美国

Traveler's cheque——旅行支票

旅行支票是一种定额支票，其作用是专供旅客购买物品和支付旅途费用的，它与一般的银行汇票、支票的不同之处在于旅行支票没有指定的付款地点和银行，一般也不受日期限制，能在全世界通用，客户可以随时在国外的各大银行、国际酒店、餐厅及其他消费场所兑换现金或直接使用，是国际旅行中常用的支付凭证之一。旅行者购买旅行支票时，需在出售银行柜台上当面在旅行支票初签位置上签字，作为预留签字，取款时，须在兑付行的柜台上当面在旅行支票的复签位置上第二次签字，兑付行核对初签与复签相符后，方可付款。因此，旅行支票遗失或被盗，不易被冒领，比携带现钞安全。

目前，全球通行的旅行支票品种有美国运通（AMERICAN EXPRESS）、VISA以及通济隆、MASTERCARD、花旗等品牌，而印有中行字样的上述旅行支票能够在世界各地800余家旅行支票代兑行兑换，或在各国的大商铺和宾馆饭店直接使用。其中美国运通旅行支票在中国大陆2000多家银行营业网点可以买到，合作银行包括农行、工行、中行、建行、光大银行、中信银行、交通银行。

看来我们的小丫使用美国运通的旅行支票是一个不错的选择哦。

第4课

第一次上课：你们好，我是小丫

情景介绍: 小丫来纽约快有一周时间了，经过这段时间的调整和准备，她已经非常期待新学期的开始了。今天是第一天上课，也许还会在课堂里结识新朋友呢。

会话1

Professor: Good morning, ladies and gentlemen. Welcome to The History of Arts. I believe you all know this is a trial lesson, which means you can decide whether you want to follow it or not after today. First of all, I'd like each of you to give a self-introduction, including any courses you have taken related to arts, so I can get a brief idea how much you've known.

Student A: Good morning, my name is Chris, majoring in Biology. I'm here because I'm always interested in arts, and I'd like to learn more about it. I've taken How Art is Understood by Professor Smith last year.

Student B: Hi, I'm Sarah, majoring in Philosophy. I believe arts is one of the foundations of people's mind. I haven't taken any relative courses yet, so I want to start with this one.

Student C: Hi, my name is James. I study English Literature. Literature comes from life and is a kind of arts. I want to learn more how they mutually influence. Last year, I published an article about the influence of Civil Rights movement on modern arts.

Professor: All right. This sounds like an interesting topic, but I assume it's way too broad to be concluded in a short article. Anyway, it's a good idea. Let's see the next student.

Ya: Good morning everyone, I'm Ya Jiang. I'm majoring in Advertising Design. I haven't taken any course related to arts yet, but I think the History of Arts is the basis to learn anything more about arts.

教授：大家上午好，欢迎你们来上艺术史这门课。相信你们都知道今天是试听课，也就是说你们在听过之后可以决定要不要选这门课。首先我想听听你们的自我介绍，包括你们以前学过的任何跟艺术有关的课程，以便我对你们的情况有个初步的了解。

学生1：上午好，我叫克里斯，是生物专业的学生。我选这门课是因为我对艺术一直很感兴趣，而且我想对其有更深的了解。去年我修了史密斯教授的如何解读艺术这门课。

学生2：大家好，我是莎拉，哲学专业。我相信艺术是人类思想的基础之一。我还没学过其他相关课程，所以想从这门课开始。

学生3：大家好，我是詹姆斯，英国文学专业。文学源于生活，同时又是艺术的一种形式。我想了解它们是如何互相影响的。去年，我发表了一篇文章，是关于民权运动对现代艺术的影响的。

教授：这样啊，听起来是个很有趣的话题，不过我个人认为这个话题太大，不适合在一篇短文里全面总结。总之，这是个很好的想法。我们来听听下一位同学的声音。

小丫：大家上午好，我是蒋小丫，广告设计专业。我还没修过其他跟艺术有关的课程，但是我觉得艺术史是学习艺术的基础。

会话2

(During the break, students are talking to each other.)

James: Hello, Ya, where are you from?

Ya: Hi, James, right? I'm from China. You can tell from my name. Are you American?

James: Yes, I am. I'm a native New Yorker.

Ya: Cool. I just came to New York a few days ago, so there are still a lot of things I don't know about New York and the United States.

James: Well, you've got plenty of time to learn those things. Like China, the States is also a big country, consisting of all kinds of culture and people.

Ya: I've heard about this before. America is a Melting Pot or a Salad Bowl. What does it mean exactly?

James: Wow, it's quite impressive that you know this. As you can tell, we have immigrants from all over the world, and they all bring their own culture and way of thinking. After so many years of development, we've learned to respect them and live with them.

Ya: I see. It sounds like the multiple ethnic groups in China. We also live peacefully together despite all sorts of differences.

James: Exactly. Have you got any friends in the States?

Ya: Yeah, my friend Tom is also a student of NYU.

James: Good for you.

（在课间，同学们互相交谈。）

詹姆斯： 小丫，你好，你是哪里人？

小丫： 你好，詹姆斯对吗？我是中国人，从我的名字上就可以判断了。你是美国人？

詹姆斯： 对，我是地道的纽约人。

小丫： 酷。我才来纽约几天，所以关于纽约甚至美国，我还有很多东西不了解。

詹姆斯： 嗯，你有足够的时间去了解这些东西。像中国一样，美国也是一个很大的国家，有不同的文化和人群。

小丫： 我以前听说过。美国是一个"大熔炉"或者"沙拉碗"，这到底是什么意思呢？

詹姆斯： 哇，这你都知道，真不错。正如你所知的，美国有世界各国来的移民，他们也把各自的文化和思维方式带到美国。历经这么多年的发展，我们已经学会了尊重不同的文化并与之和平共处。

小丫： 我明白了。听起来就像中国的众多少数民族。我们也求同存异地和平共处。

詹姆斯： 这正是我想说的。你在美国有朋友吗？

小丫： 有，我的朋友汤姆也是纽约大学的学生。

詹姆斯： 真有你的。

必备词汇

brief adj.

简略的，简短的，简洁的

例如 The professor did a brief evaluation. 教授做了一个简单的评价。Students need to make the content relevant and brief when writing. 学生在写作时需要保证内容切题并且简要。

foundation n.

基础，根据，（建筑物的）地基

例如 Truth is the foundation of freedom. 真理是自由的基础。The foundation of the building is firm. 这座楼房的地基牢固。

conclude v.

总结，归纳，结束

例如 To conclude, using public transport is good for the environment. 综上所述，使用公共交通对环境有益。The meeting is going to conclude on Sunday. 会议将在周日结束。

ethnic group

民族，种族群体

例如 There are fifty-six ethnic groups in China. 中国有56个民族。

mutual adj.

互相的，彼此的

例如 Mutual understanding is very important to friendship. 相互理解对友谊非常重要。

influence n.

影响，作用，影响力

另外也有v.影响，感化，左右。**例如** Mr. Smith is a man of influence in the city. 史密斯先生是这座城市中有影响力的人。The plants are strongly influenced by the weather. 植物深受天气的影响。

major v.

主修，和介词in搭配使用。

另外也有n.专业，主修科目，主修学生。
例如 He majors (v.) in English Literature. 他是英国文学专业。同样可以表达为His major（n.）is English Literature. 他的专业是英国文学。

include v.

包括，包含

用法较多，注意下面例子中的不同形式。
例如 Does the price include tax? 这个价钱包括税款吗？ You need to fill in your personal information, including your age, gender, profession and so on. 你需要填入个人信息，包括年龄、性别和职业等。The cost of the traffic is included in the price. 交通费已经包含在价格里了。

multiple adj.

多重的，多样的，多个的

例如 He had multiple achievements on music. 他在音乐上有多样的成就。multiple choice 选择题。

native adj.

本土的，本地的；n.本地人，本国人

例如 My native language is Chinese. 汉语是我的本国语言。He is a native of New York. 他是纽约本地人。

break n.

暂停，休息

v.打破，毁坏，破碎
例如 There is a ten-minute break between the classes. 课间有十分钟的休息时间。

trial n.

试用，试验，尝试

例如 This shop provides free trial to new customers. 这家店为新客户提供免费试用。

despite prep.

不管，尽管，任凭

例如 They stay friends despite all their differences. 尽管看法不同，他们依然保持好朋友的关系。

related adj.

有关的，相关的

例如 To do this job, you need at least 2 years of related working experience. 做这项工作，你需要两年以上相关的工作经验。

地道美语

① Give me a break. 饶了我吧。／让我静静吧。／让我休息一下。本课中出现了during the break这个词组，跟break同义的俚语Give me a break也是美国人日常对话中经常出现的。如果对方说了让你无法相信或者无法接受的话，可以这样回应。例如：

Roommate: You always leave things everywhere in the house, but you never clean up. You know, I need to study, too. This is not fair…

Thomas: Give me a break, please. What you are saying is not true, and I have a lot of work to do now!

宝友：　你总是把东西扔的到处都是，但是你从来不打扫。你要知道，我也需要学习。这是不公平的……

托马斯：　让我静一静吧。你说的不对，并且我现在有很多事情要做！

---

② **Good for you.** 很不错。/ 真有你的。用在对方(将要或已经)做一件对自己有益的事时，所表示"认同"的话。例如：

A: I'm going to join a swimming club and a football club. I feel like doing some sports.

B: Good for you. When will you start?

A：我要参加一个游泳俱乐部和一个足球俱乐部。我想做些运动。

B：不错啊！你打算什么时候开始？

feel like doing sth 想要做某事。例如：

I feel like seeing a science fiction film tonight.
我今晚想看一部科幻电影。

---

③ **It's way too...** "太……"是美式口语中很常见的表达方式，这里的 way 是 adv. 副词，意为"太，很多"，在副词或副词词组前面使用。学会了这种用法，就不会出现 I drink very too much coffee. 这样的 Chinglish 表达方式啦。例如：

They are driving way too fast. It's way too dangerous.
他们车开得太快了，这样太危险了。

This party is way out of our budget.
这场晚会远远超出我们的预算。

有一部美国喜剧电影《She's Out of My League》(《我配不上她》)，里面男主角的一句台词是：She's way out of my league. 我远配不上她。也是日常对话中实用的美国俚语。例如：

A: I really want to date that blond girl in my school.
B: You wish man. She's way out of your league.

A：我真想跟学校里的金发美女约会。
B：你倒是想。你远配不上她。

④ Ladies and gentlemen. 女士们，先生们。在西方国家，尤其是英美，一些大学老师和大学教授对学生表现出成年人之间的尊重，以先生和小姐称呼。例如：

Professor: Would you answer this question, Mr Williams?
教授：你可以回答这个问题吗，威廉姆斯先生？

Presenter: Ladies and gentlemen, you are the future of our school.
主持人：女士们先生们，你们是我校的未来。

⑤ Melting Pot./ Salad Bowl 种族混杂的国家。Melting pot和salad bowl原意分别为"大熔炉"和"沙拉碗"，后引申为种族混杂的国家，特指美国。相比之下，melting pot更为生动形象，也更为常用。例如：

New York city is the most famous Melting Pot in the world.
纽约是世界上最有名的各色人种混杂的地方。

⑥ New Yorker 纽约人。英语中习惯在城市名称的基础上直接变换形式，使之成为……人，类似的还有Londoner，Shanghainese等。同时，The New Yorker（《纽约客》）也是美国著名的综合文艺类刊物。例如：

Although he spent his entire life in Paris, he's still a
New Yorker in the heart.

> 尽管他的一生都在巴黎度过，但内心深处他仍然
> 是一个纽约人。

7 plyenty of time **大量的时间**。plenty of...**是美国人口语中常**
用的词组，比如plenty of time, plenty of water, plenty of
good books，**既可以和可数名词搭配使用，也可以和不可**
数名词搭配使用，类似的表达方式还有a bunch of，**意为**
"一大帮，一大群"，但仅和可数名词搭配使用。例如：

I need plenty of time to prepare for the exams.

> 我需要大量的时间来准备考试。

I have a whole bunch of friends to visit this summer.

> 今年夏天我有一大群朋友要去拜访。

表达方式百宝箱

　　本课中出现了课堂用语及和新同学交流时所用到的表达
方式，现在就让我们来总结一下吧！

Give me a break. 饶了我吧。／让我静静吧。／让我休息
一下。

Good for you. 真有你的！／真不错！

I'm Chris, majoring in Biology. 我是克莉丝，生物学专业。

James is a native New Yorker. 詹姆斯是纽约本地人。

Ladies and gentlemen. 女士们先生们。

Let's see the next student. 让我们听听下一位同学。

She's way out of my league. 我远配不上她。

You've got plenty of time to learn those things. 你有很多的
时间去了解这些东西。

小丫 **带你走遍美国**

New York University (NYU)——纽约大学

纽约大学（New York University，简称NYU），成立于1831年，是全美最大的私立大学之一，也是美国唯一一座坐落于纽约心脏地带的名校。作为一所世界一流的学术机构，纽约大学拥有33名诺贝尔奖获得者、3名阿贝尔奖得主、21名奥斯卡奖、艾美奖、格莱美奖和东尼奖得主、9名美国国家科学勋章获得者、16名普利策奖获得者以及19名美国科学院勋章获得者。纽约大学所设课程压力不大，但要求甚高，学生称其为"not high pressure, but demanding"。纽约大学较为偏重人文艺术及社会科学，曾出过12位首级人物，另外如Lady Gaga、小约翰·菲茨杰拉德·肯尼迪、辜振甫、陈履安、马英九等名人也皆为纽约大学的毕业校友。

纽约大学共有18个学院及6个中心分布于曼哈顿，其中大学部设有4个学院及80余系及各种系际合作的课程；研究所则有11个学院75系，所提供的课程超过25000种，而所提供的学位也有25种之多。研究所偏重于人文、社会及艺术方面的人才培养，一般说来（除一些特殊科系外），各研究学院均同时提供硕士及博士的课程。其中还包括海外进修课程，例如欧洲、南美洲的暑期课程，以及去医院实习的机会或参与其他社会实践的机会，课程的安排多元而丰富，大致倾向于实用、以应用为主。

看来，我们的小丫选择纽约大学是明智之举，还可以和众多各界名人成为校友呢。

第5课

快递先锋：我错拿了妈妈的身份证

情景介绍 小丫周末在家收拾行李，突然发现妈妈的身份证夹在自己的证件包中。上次跟妈妈视频聊天的时候妈妈没有提起这件事，说明妈妈还不知道呢。想到这儿小丫开始着急了，但是又不知道怎么办才好，便打通了汤姆的电话……

会话1

Tom: Hello, this is Tom Hunters.

Ya: Hello, Tom. This is Ya. I have an emergency.

Tom: Hey, Ya, slow down. What happened?

Ya: I found my mom's ID card in my suitcase, and I can't call her now because of the time difference. Can you help me?

Tom: Sure. Let me see. I think the best now is to send it back to your mom and then call her when it's daytime in China. What about sending an express?

Ya: It's a great idea, but how can I send an express?

Tom: We have several express services, such as FedEx, UPS, TNT and DHL. I prefer FedEx, because they are fast of course, and you can really trust them.

Ya: Ok, then I shall also try FedEx, but I don't know how to send it. I've never used express service before.

Tom: I have time today, so maybe I can come over and help you out.

Ya: That will be perfect! Thank you so much.

(About half an hour later, the door bell rings…)

Ya: You are very fast. Come on in.

Tom: You don't live that far, plus I have a bike. Before I left, I quickly searched the phone number of the FedEx closest to your neighborhood. Let's try it out.

Ya: Right. A friend in need is a friend indeed. Thank you for the help.

汤姆：你好，我是汤姆·亨特。

小丫：你好，汤姆，我是小丫，我有一件急事。

汤姆：嗨，小丫。慢点说，怎么了？

小丫：我在行李箱里发现了妈妈的身份证，因为时差我又不能现在告诉她。你能帮帮我吗？

汤姆： 当然了。让我想想。我觉得现在最好的办法是把身份证先寄回给你妈妈，然后在中国是白天的时候打电话告诉她。寄个快递怎么样？

小丫： 这个主意真棒！但是我怎么寄快递呢？

汤姆： 这边有几家快递公司，比如联邦快递、UPS、TNT和敦豪。我比较喜欢联邦快递，首先当然是因为他们比较快，也是因为他们很可靠。

小丫： 好的，那我也试试联邦快递吧，但我还是不知道怎么寄，我以前从来没寄过快递。

汤姆： 今天我有时间，或许我可以过来帮你。

小丫： 那最完美了。非常感谢！

（大约半小时以后，门铃响了……）

小丫： 你真快。快进来吧。

汤姆： 你住的没那么远，而且我有自行车。出门之前，我迅速查了一下离你家最近的联邦快递的联系电话。我们试试看。

小丫： 好的。患难之交才是真朋友啊。太谢谢你帮忙了。

会话2

Service hotline: Good morning, this is FedEx Express. May I help you?

Tom: Yes, my friend would like to send an express to China.

Service hotline: I see. Wait a second. I'm going to put you on the line to my colleague who's in charge of sending.

Tom: That's good. Thank you.

(Tom softly said to Ya: I'm gonna put it on loud speaker.)

FedEx staff: Good morning, FedEx Express. May I help you?

Tom: Yes, please. My friend and I wanna send an express to China.

FedEx: Yes. What will be the subject?

Tom: It's only an ID card. Can you tell us how long it will take and the cost?

FedEx: It will take normally 3 to 4 days to arrive in China, and the cost for sending the ID card will be 93 dollars. If you want to send it with the Extra Express service, it will take maximum 3 days and it costs 20 dollars more.

Tom: I see. I think we will go for the normal service. Do you come and get it or do we need to bring the envelop to your office?

FedEx: We don't provide fetching service, so you will need to come to our office. Sorry for the trouble.

Tom: That's no trouble. We will go to the office this afternoon. Thank you for the information.

FedEx: You are welcome. Have a nice day. Bye.

Tom: You, too. Bye.

Ya: It's not as complicated as I expected. We shall go to their office then.

Tom: Sure. Let's go now.

服务热线： 上午好，这里是联邦快递，有什么可以帮助您的？

汤姆： 是的，我朋友想寄一个快递去中国。

服务热线： 我知道了。稍等，我把电话转给负责寄快递的同事。

汤姆： 好的，谢谢。

（汤姆悄悄地对小丫说：我把免提打开。）

联邦快递工作人员： 上午好，联邦快递，有什么可以帮助您？

汤姆： 是的，我跟我朋友想寄一个快递去中国。

联邦快递工作人员： 好的，寄的是什么呢？

汤姆： 只有一个身份证。能告诉我需要多长时间寄到并且费用是多少吗？

联邦快递工作人员： 寄到中国大概需要3到4天，只寄身份证的费用是93美元。如果您想使用加快服务的话，最多3天时间寄到，但是你需要多支付20美元。

汤姆： 我知道了。我想我们还是用普通服务吧。是你们过来取件还是我们需要把信封送到你们办公室？

联邦快递工作人员: 我们不提供取件服务，所以你们要自己来办公室。给您添麻烦了，不好意思。

汤姆: 不麻烦。我们今天下午就去你们的办公室。谢谢您提供的信息。

联邦快递工作人员: 不客气。祝您度过愉快的一天。再见。

汤姆: 您也一样。再见。

小丫: 不像我想象的那么复杂。那我们这就去他们的办公室吧。

汤姆: 好的，我们现在就走吧。

必备词汇

time difference

时差

同义的说法还有jet lag。其中有细微的区别，time difference强调客观事实，jet lag更偏向主观感受，请大家注意下面两个例子的对比。**例如** What is the time difference between Beijing and New York? 北京和纽约的时差是多少？I still have jet lag for a week after travelling overseas. 我出国旅游一周后还有时差。

emergency [ɪˈməːdʒənsi] n.

紧急情况，突发事件，非常时刻

日常生活中遇到的急事便可以说成"emergency"。

例如 Call the police in the event of emergency. 在紧急情况下给警察打电话。

daytime
['deitaim] n.

白天
反义词是night n. 夜晚，晚上。

例 如 We have to get to that city in the daytime. 我们必须在白天到达那座城市。Some people work more efficiently at night than in the daytime. 有些人晚上比白天工作更加有效率。

express
[ik'spres] n.

快递
跟我们平时知道的（v. 表达）可不是一个意思哦。

例 如 I need to send this express immediately. 我需要马上寄出这个快递。

fetch
[fetʃ] v.

拿，取

例 如 We will send someone to fetch your things. 我们会派人去把你的东西取来。

loud speaker

扩音器，扬声器
也就是我们电话和手机上的"免提"。

例 如 Jack turned on the loud speaker so his family can hear the good news. 杰克打开了免提，以便家人可以听到这个好消息。

suitcase
['sju:tkeis] n.

手提箱，衣箱，旅行箱
旅行中必不可少的装备之一。

例 如 She packed her clothes into her suitcase. 她把衣服装进了旅行箱。

complicated
['kɔmplikeitid] adj.

复杂的，难懂的

例如 This is a very complicated problem.
这是一个非常复杂的问题。

neighborhood
['neibəhud] n.

邻近地区，街道

例如 The shop has put up many advertisement throughout the neighborhood. 这家商店在邻近地区张贴了许多广告。

service hotline
['hɔtlain] n.

服务热线

在网站和快递公司的页面上都会显示服务热线，也方便顾客与之联系。

例如 The service hotline of this company is available 24 hours a day. 这家公司的服务热线每天24小时开通。

staff
[stɑːf, stæf] n.

工作人员，员工

例如 Some of our staff will retire this year. 我们一些员工今年会退休。

地道美语

① A friend in need is a friend indeed. 患难见真情。／患难朋友才是真正的朋友。这是一句经典的英语俗语，和汉语的"患难见真情"可谓异曲同工。例如：

A: Thank you so much for helping me out of the big trouble. I don't know how to pay you back.

B: Don't be silly. A friend in need is a friend indeed.

> A：真是太感谢你了，救我于水火之中，我都不知道如何报答你。
>
> B：别傻了。患难朋友才是真正的朋友啊。

例子中出现的Don't be silly，也是美式口语中常见的表达方式。类似于汉语中的"别说傻话了"。有对对方的怜爱之意。例如：

A: You are too good for me. I'm not the same kind of person as you.

B: Don't be silly. I love you because of you, nothing else.

> A：你对我来说太好了，我们不是一路人。
>
> B：别傻了。我爱的就是你，不是其他任何东西。

❷ I can come over and help you out. 我可以过来帮你。此句中出现的come over和help you out是很口语化的说法，分别意为"过来"和"帮忙"。例如：

A: It's been a long time since I saw you last time. Maybe you can come over this weekend?

B: I've been extremely busy the last few weeks, but I will make some time for my mom.

> A：从我上次看见你到现在有很长时间了。要不你这周末过来一趟？

B: 上几周我特别忙，但是为了妈妈，我一定抽出时间过去。

A: Mom, I have a big problem here, can you help me out?

B: Sure, honey. I'll be right there.

    A: 妈妈，我这出了个大问题，你能来帮我解决吗？

    B: 当然了，亲爱的。我马上就到。

例句中出现的I'll be right there，也是美国人常用的口语表发，类似说法还有I'm on my way，都意为"我马上就到"。例如：

A: Where are you now? The party will start in 10 minutes.

B: I'll be right there.

    A: 你现在到哪儿了？晚会还有十分钟就开始了。

    B: 我马上就到。

---

③ Let me see. 让我想想。／让我看看。在遇到问题或者有所犹豫时会使用这种表达方式，意为"稍等，我想想"。例如：

A: I don't know how to solve this problem. It's getting too complicated.

B: Let me see. I'm sure we will find a way.

    A: 我不知道怎么解决这个问题。它变得很复杂。

    B: 让我想想，我们一定会找出一个办法的。

④ **Slow down.** 放慢，减缓，在文中意为"慢点说"。在对方比较焦急的时候也是安慰对方的一种表达方式。或者用字面意思，在对方开车超速时告诫对方要减速。例如：

A: I have so much to do. I need to pick up Jenny after school, I need to prepare for the family dinner, I need to…

B: Hey, slow down. I will give you a hand.

> A: 我有太多事要做了，要接珍妮放学，要准备家庭聚会晚餐，还要……
>
> B: 嗨，别着急，我会帮你的。

例句中出现的**give sb a hand** 是帮忙之意。例如：

I really don't have the time to do that. Can you give me a hand?

> 我真没时间去做那件事，你能帮帮我吗？

---

⑤ **Sorry for the trouble.** 对不起，给你添麻烦了。是在需要对方帮忙或者打扰对方之后表达歉意的说法。例如：

A: Sorry for the trouble. I ask you to help every time I have a problem.

B: No problem. I'm always ready to help you.

> A: 对不起，给你添麻烦了。每次有问题我都来找你帮忙。
>
> B: 没问题，我随时都愿意帮助你。

---

⑥ **We will go for the normal service.** 我们还是选择普通服务吧。**go for** 意为"选择，倾向，喜欢"。比起**choose**或者**take**更加口语化，也更受年轻人欢迎。例如：

A: I'm gonna take a beer. Would you like a beer?

B: No, thanks. I think I'll go for a coffee.

A: 我要喝杯啤酒，你也要杯啤酒吗？

B: 不用了，谢谢。我想我还是喝咖啡吧。

表达方式百宝箱

现在，让我们来总结一下本课中学习过的表达方式吧。

A friend in need is a friend indeed. 患难朋友才是真正的朋友。

Can you give me a hand? 你能帮帮我吗？

Don't be silly. 别傻了。

I can come over and help you out. 我可以过来帮你。

I'll be right there. 我马上就到。

Let me see. 让我想想。

Slow down. 慢点说，别着急。

Sorry for the trouble. 对不起，给你添麻烦了。

We will go for the normal service. 我们还是用普通服务吧。

小丫 带你走遍美国

FedEx（联邦快递）——美国最大的快递公司

联邦快递是一家国际性速递集团，提供隔夜快递、地面快递、重型货物运送、文件复印及物流服务，总部设于美国田纳西州。其品牌商标FedEx是由公司原来的英文名称Federal Express合并而成。

联邦快递在1971年由前美国海军陆战队队员Frederick W. Smith（弗雷德·W·史密斯）在阿肯色州小石城创立，但在1973年迁往田纳西州孟菲斯。联邦快递迁往田纳西州后为25个城市提供服务，但困难重重，初期出现严重亏损，但数年后，业务开始有所改善。到了1975年7月，公司首度出现盈利。1978年，联邦快递正式上市。

进入70世纪60年代以后，美国经济越来越依赖服务业和高技术产业，对那些从事技术的公司或者依赖信息的公司来说，传统的邮政传递和货运公司在可靠性和时效性上都远远不能满足他们的要求。于是在美国的运输市场上，急需一种能够保证快速、可靠地传送货物的公司出现。这是时代的挑战，更是难得的机遇。然而，敏锐地发现这一机遇，并勇敢地接受挑战，紧紧把握历史契机的，就是被誉为"隔夜快递业之父"的美国著名企业家——弗雷德·W·史密斯。他在美国历史上首创了"隔夜快递"这一新兴的服务行业。

当然，有市场就必然有竞争，联邦快递的最大竞争对手有DHL、UPS和美国邮政。

单车游纽约

情景介绍: 小丫来纽约有段时间了,但一直没有机会观光,对于自己学习和生活的纽约市还是感觉有些陌生。恰好今天杰瑞和汤姆都有时间,三个人约好了一起单车游纽约。

会话1

Tom: Ya, you have been in New York for a while. How much do you know about the city now?

Ya: Honestly, I don't know much about New York, because I haven't got the time to walk around.

Jerry: What a shame. Fortunately, we all have time today. Why don't we bike around New York and give you a city tour?

Tom: Yeah, fantastic! I'm in! What do you say, Ya?

Ya: Of course I like it. But I don't have a bike. What about you guys?

Jerry: You know in a metropolis like New York, people don't really bike, and it's not easy to bike here with all the traffic. But we've got bikes anyway, and Jessica has a bike, too. She's not going to use it today, so we can borrow hers.

Tom: Good idea! Why don't we call her now to ask?

Jerry: Wait a minute. I'm going to call her.

(Jerry and Jessica talking on the phone...)

Jerry: Jessica agreed. Her bike is in her apartment, but she's not at home right now. Luckily I have a spare key to her place, so we can go there now.

Tom: You see, it's sometimes good to have a girlfriend.

Jerry: Ya, forget what he just said. He's jealous of me.

Ya: Close friends always make fun of each other. I do the same with my friends.

汤姆： 小丫，你来纽约也有一段时间了。现在对纽约了解得怎么样了？

小丫： 说实话，我对纽约还不是很了解，因为我没有时间到处走走看看。

杰瑞： 真遗憾！不过幸运的是我们今天都有时间，要不然我们骑车转转纽约给你当导游？

汤姆： 对呀，妙极了！我同意。小丫你觉得呢？

小丫： 我当然喜欢这个主意啦！不过我没有自行车，你们有吗？

杰瑞： 你知道吗？其实在像纽约这样的大都市人们一般不骑自行车，而且在这种交通情况下骑车也不容易。但是，我们还是有自行车的，杰西卡也有自行车。反正她今天也用不着，所以我们可以先借她的。

汤姆： 好主意！为什么我们不现在就问问她呢？

杰瑞： 稍等。我这就问问她。

（杰瑞和杰西卡在电话中交谈……）

杰瑞： 杰西卡同意了。她的自行车在她的公寓里，可是她现在不在家。还好我有她家的钥匙，所以我们现在就可以过去。

汤姆： 你看，有个女朋友有时还是不错的。

杰瑞： 小丫，他刚说的你就当没听见。他是嫉妒我。

小丫： 好朋友总是开对方的玩笑。我和我的朋友们也这样。

会话2

(After getting the bike for Ya in Jessica's apartment...)

Jerry: There is a great deal to see in New York, so much that it's impossible to do everything in one day, so I propose we make a must-see list and stick to it.

Tom: Yeah, Jerry's right. We've got museums, grand hotels, amusement parks, skyscrapers, historical spots and many other things. What interest you?

Ya: Wow, basically all of them! If I have to make a choice, I will go for museums and historical spots. I've always been interested in arts and history.

Tom: Perfect! Jerry and I will try to be good guides for you.

Jerry: We can first go to MOMA, the art works there are amazing!

Ya: What is MOMA?

Jerry: MOMA is the Museum of Modern Art, which locates at 11 West 53rd Street. Jessica likes it a lot, but it took me two visits before I started to like it. I wonder what you will think about the art there.

Tom: MOMA is a nice place, but we are going to bike around instead of appreciating art works, right?

Ya: Yeah, Tom is right. Anyway I'd like to visit MOMA with you and Jessica when you have time, Jerry.

Jerry: All right then. We shall go see churches. They are the perfect combination of art and history! The best will be the Trinity Church on Broadway.

Tom: Genius idea! We can pass by on our bikes and take a look at the architecture style.

Ya: Sounds great to me! Let's head for Trinity Church!

（在杰西卡的公寓帮小丫取完自行车以后……）

杰瑞： 纽约有很多好看的东西，太多了，以至于我们不可能在一天之内看完所有的东西，所以我提议我们列一个"必看"清单，然后按照单子里的内容安排。

汤姆： 对，杰瑞说得对。我们有博物馆、大酒店、游乐园、摩天大楼、历史古迹，还有许多其他的东西。你对什么感兴趣呢？

小丫： 哇！基本上这些我都感兴趣。不过如果一定要做出选择，那我选博物馆和历史古迹，我一直对艺术和历史感兴趣。

汤姆： 太好了！我和杰瑞会努力做好导游的。

杰瑞： 我们可以先去MOMA，那儿的艺术作品棒极了。

小丫： MOMA是什么？

杰瑞： MOMA是现代艺术博物馆，坐落于西53大街11号。杰西卡特别喜欢这座博物馆，不过我是去了两次才开始喜欢它的。我好奇你怎么看那儿的现代艺术。

汤姆： MOMA是个好地方，但是我们今天要单车转纽约，而不是欣赏艺术，不是吗？

小丫： 对哦，汤姆说得对。不过杰瑞，我很有兴趣参观MOMA，如果你和杰西卡什么时候有时间，我们一起去吧。

杰瑞： 那好吧。我们应该去参观教堂，它们是艺术和历史的最完美结合。最好的选择莫过于百老汇的圣三一教堂了。

汤姆： 天才！我们可以骑车转转，并看看它的建筑风格。

小丫： 听起来好极了！我们现在就向圣三一教堂出发吧。

必备词汇

amusement park
[ə'mju:zmənt] n.

游乐场，游乐园

我们熟知的Disney Land（迪士尼乐园）和欢乐谷都是这一类。另外theme park是主题公园，专门用于形容像迪士尼乐园这样有一定主题的游乐园。**例如** Children can go wild in amusement parks. 孩子们在游乐园里可以尽情玩耍。

appreciate
[ə'pri:ʃieit] v.

欣赏，赏识，鉴赏

宾语除了艺术作品和文艺作品之外，还可以是人。**例如** Her abilities are not fully appreciated by her boss. 她的才能尚未得到老板的充分赏识。

architecture
['ɑ:kitektʃə] n.

建筑，建筑设计，建筑风格

和building对比，更加抽象、概括，强调整体概念。**例如** Beijing is famous for its architecture. 北京以其建筑闻名。Architecturally Chengdu is quite different from most of China. 从建筑学角度来看，成都和中国的大部分城市不一样。

jealous
['dʒeləs] adj.

嫉妒的，吃醋的

本文中因为汤姆和杰瑞是好朋友，所以并无贬义。**例如** He is so jealous of her success. 他是如此嫉妒她的成就。

combination
[ˌkɔmbiˈneiʃ ən] n.

结合，联合，混合

可以用于指代具体名词和抽象名词。课文中出现的the perfect combination of art and history就是指代抽象名词。**例如** a perfect wine and food combination 美酒佳肴的完美组合，便是指代具体名词。

fantastic
[fænˈtæstik] adj.

极好的，吸引人的，有趣的

可以用于修饰人或者物。**例如** You look fantastic! 你的气色好极了！This idea sounds fantastic to me. 我觉得这个主意棒极了。名词形式是fantasy，意为幻想，想象。著名歌手周杰伦曾经出过一本专辑名为《范特西》，便来源于此。**例如** Young children sometimes can't distinguish between fatasy and reality. 小孩子有时不能区分幻想与现实。

fortunately
[ˈfɔːtʃ ənitli] adv.

幸运地，幸亏

例如 Fortunately the fire was discovered soon after it started. 幸运的是，火刚着了不久就被发现了。名词形式是fortune，意为"财富，运气，命运"。形容词形式是fortunate，意为"幸运的，偶然发生的，巧合的"。**例如** They must have spent a fortune on that house. 他们买那栋房子肯定花了一大笔钱。You are fortunate that you still got a job. 你真幸运，仍然有一份工作。

grand
[grænd] adj.

宏伟的，壮观的，盛大的

例如 They had a grand wedding last week. 他们上周举办了一场盛大的婚礼。

metropolis
[mi'trɔpəlis, me-] n.

（一国或地区的）首要城市，大都会

例如 New York is indeed a metropolis. 纽约是个名副其实的大都会。

propose
[prəu'pəuz] v.

提议，建议，提出

例如 David has proposed that I become his business partner. 大卫提议我成为他的生意合伙人。

skyscraper
['skai,skreipə] n.

摩天大楼

例如 The famous skyscraper "The World Trade Center" was attacked by terrorists a few years ago. 著名的摩天大楼"世贸大厦"几年前遭到了恐怖组织的袭击。

while
[hwail] n

一段时间，一会儿

while的这个词性和我们熟知的连词（当……时，与……同时发生）有很大不同，请注意区分。

例如 They came in while we were having dinner. 他们进来的时候，我们正在吃晚饭。（连词）Bob has only been working here for a short while. 鲍勃在这里只工作了一小段时间。（名词）

honestly
['ɔnistli] adv.

诚实地，正直地；真的，的确

例如 Honestly! Can't you find better things to do with your time? 真不像话，你难道不能做些更好的事来打发时间吗？Honestly, I don't know how to answer your question. 说实话，我不知道怎么回答你的问题。

impossible
[im'pɔsəbl] adj.

不可能发生的，办不到的

反义词是possible，意为可能发生的，办得到的。例如 It's impossible to finish this program in time. 不可能按时完成这个项目。It is possible that he will be the next winner. 他有可能成为下一个赢家。

地道美语

① Close friends always make fun of each other. **好朋友总是互相开玩笑。** 需要注意的词组为make fun of，意为嘲笑某人／某物，拿某人／某物开玩笑。例如：

A: He looks like a clown in that sweater.

B: It's not nice making fun of people's looks.

　A: 他穿那件毛衣看起来像个小丑。

　B: 拿别人的外表开玩笑可不好。

A: I'm going to a party this evening. Do you want to join?

B: I think I'll watch a movie at home. Have fun!

A：我今晚要去参加个晚会，你要一起来吗？

B：我想我还是在家看个电影吧。你玩得开心哦！

例句中出现的"Have fun!"也是常用口语表达，意为祝对方玩得愉快。

---

2 **I haven't got the time to walk around.** 我还没时间到处转转。句中the time特指为walk around (到处走走)的时间，所以使用定冠词the。

---

3 **Walk on eggs/ eggshells** 意为（对易怒的人）小心翼翼，如履薄冰。例如：

A: I've been walking on eggs for several weeks. My boss is having a hard time with his boss.

B: I totally understand. Better not make him angry.

A：我这几周都是如履薄冰，我上司正跟他上司闹得很不愉快。

B：我完全理解。最好不要惹他生气。

---

4 **I propose we make a must-see list and stick to it.** 我提议我们列一个"必看"清单，然后按照单子上的内容安排。must-do意为"必做"，stick to意为"坚持，坚守，遵守"。例如：

A: It's the first time I eat Chinese food. Do you have any suggestions for me?

B: Well, hot pot is a must-eat in China.

A：这是我第一次中餐，你有什么建议吗？

B：嗯，火锅是来中国必吃的。

A: Why do we need to stick to the rules all the time? Can't we be original?

B: You can be original on the condition of sticking to the rules.

A: 为什么我们一定要遵守规则？不能有点创新吗？

B: 你可以在遵守规则的基础上创新。

⑤ **I'm in! 我同意！/我加入！这是美语中既简洁又常用的表达方式。完整表达为be/ get in on sth 参与某事。使用时on sth多省略。例如：**

A: I'm interested in the coming Campus Debate. Who wants to be on my side?

B: I'm in!

A: 我对最近要开始的校园辩论会很有兴趣，谁愿意跟我一组？

B: 我加入！

例句中be on one's side意为站在某人一边，口语中常用whose side are you on? 你究竟站在哪一边？用于某人本该支持你，却发表了反对你的意见。例如：

A: Whose side are you on? You are speaking for him!

B: Sorry buddy, I think he's got a bigger chance.

A: 你究竟站在哪一边？怎么替他说话！

B: 对不起兄弟，我觉得他的机会更大。

6 Let's head for Trinity Church! 我们现在就向圣三一教堂出发吧！注意句中的head for，意为"向……去，朝……前进"。例如：

A: Where are you guys heading for?
B: We are going to get drunk.

A: 你们要去哪儿？
B: 我们要去喝个一醉方休。

7 Strike while the iron is hot. 趁热打铁。while在本句中的词性便是连词，和本课中所学的名词词性不同。例如：

A: You have been practicing the violin for three hours. Don't you take a break?
B: Well, I need to strike while the iron is hot. I just had a lesson this morning.

A: 你已经练了三个小时的小提琴了，都不休息一会儿吗？
B: 哎呀，我要趁热打铁。今天上午刚上过课。

8 There is a great deal to see in New York. 在纽约要看的有很多。注意句中的a great deal，意为"很多的，大量的"。同义还有a good deal。例如：

A great deal of their work is unpaid.
他们的很多工作都没有报酬。

另外涉及deal的美语中常用的还有It's a deal! 意为成交（同意做某事）。例如：

Mom: Let's make a deal. You wash the car, and we will pay you by hour. Ok?

Son: It's a deal!

> 妈妈：我们来做个交易。你来洗车，然后我和爸爸按小时付费。好不好？
>
> 儿子：成交！

⑨ **What a shame.** 多遗憾啊。我们以前学过what a pity，但这种说法已经有点过时了，相比之下，what a shame更加地道。注意shame在这里并不是"可耻"的意思。例如：

A: I have been to Tokyo many times, but they were all business trips, so I never had the chance to see the city.

B: What a shame! You should go there for a holiday.

> A：我已经去过好几次东京了，不过都是因公出差，所以从来没有时间参观这座城市。
>
> B：多遗憾啊！你应该到东京度个假。

⑩ **What do you say?** 你觉得怎么样？比起我们以前学过的how do you like it?或者what do you think about it?是不是简单也地道很多呢？例如：

A: What do you say we throw a party?

B: Why not? Let's do it!

> A：你觉得我们办个晚会怎么样？
>
> B：为什么不呢？我们就办一场吧！

表达方式百宝箱

本课中，在三个主人公讨论如何单车游纽约的时候，用到了很多地道的美语表达方式，现在就让我们一起来总结一下吧！

Close friends always make fun of each other. 好朋友总是互相开玩笑。

Have fun! 玩得愉快！

I haven't got the time to walk around. 我没有时间到处走走看看。

I'm in! 我同意！/我加入！

Let's head for Trinity Church! 我们现在就向圣三一教堂出发吧！

Ya, you have been in New York for a while. 小丫，你来纽约有段时间了。

There is a great deal to see in New York. 在纽约要看的有很多。

Walk on eggs/ eggshells. （对易怒的人）小心翼翼，如履薄冰。

What a shame. 多遗憾啊。

What do you say? 你觉得怎么样？

Whose side are you on? 你究竟站在哪一边？

小丫 带你走遍 美国

纽约圣三一教堂——艺术和历史的完美结合

美国纽约圣三一教堂位于华尔街的西街口，紧临百老汇大街，可以说是一座典型的哥特式教堂。在19世纪初它曾经是纽约最高的建筑，是它见证了华尔街风风雨雨的历史。在教堂西侧有一小块墓地，这里安葬着很多知名的金融大亨和政治名人。如果华尔街的大亨们按照常规拿出自己收入的10%捐给教堂的话，那么这座三一教堂无疑是世界上最富有的教堂。

圣三一是基督教教义中的重要概念，所以在很多西方宗教国家都有圣三一教堂。在我国上海也有圣三一教堂。它是英国圣公会在上海的一座教堂，俗称红礼拜堂。该教堂位于黄浦区，东面是江西中路，西面到九江路，南面到汉口路。这是一座专门为英国侨民服务的教堂，1847年建成，1866年5月24日-1869年重新建造，外围为哥特式，成为上海早期最大最华丽的基督教堂。由斯科特·凯德纳设计。1875年升格为北华教区主教堂，1893年教堂左侧增建高耸的钟楼（已毁于文化大革命中）。这里长期作为黄浦区政府。最终会还给教会，作为中国基督教两会所在地。

可见，教堂真的是历史与艺术的完美融合啊。

第7课

情景介绍： 每个远渡重洋出国留学的学生都要面临的问题便是衣食住行，来到陌生的国家，语言和环境都有很大的差异。住又是首先要解决的问题，不仅需要考虑到房间的位置，交通是否便利，治安是否良好，还要考虑到房内的设施，也许还有室友要面对。下面就来看看我们的小丫是如何面对住房问题的吧。

会话1

Ya: I'm fed up with my hostel room. It's time for me to look for an apartment.

Tom: Yeah, I know. Living in an apartment gives you more space and freedom. But the good thing about the hostel is that you don't need to clean the room.

Ya: You are right, but I don't really mind cleaning the room, and I want to be able to decorate my own room.

Tom: That's a fair reason. Then you definitely should get an apartment.

Ya: The problem is that I don't know anything about the location or the price.

Tom: That's no problem. Don't worry. We can sort it out, otherwise we can always google it.

Ya: We have the same in China. It's called Baidu, but we call it "Du Niang" which means Lady Du. Most Chinese people prefer Baidu than Google.

Tom: I've heard of it, but it's not so popular here.

Ya: Where do you live? I never asked where you and Jerry live? Is it close to the school?

Tom: It's pretty far. I mean it's like 15 minutes on foot.

Ya: You call that far? Back in China, I walked more than 15 minutes everyday to school.

Tom: All right, so you are all prepared.

Ya: Sure. Let's get started on the details.

小丫： 我住够青年旅社的房间了，我觉得是时候要找个公寓住了。

汤姆： 是啊，我理解。住公寓的话给你更多的空间跟自由，但是住青年旅社有一点好处就是你不需要自己打扫房间。

小丫： 你说得对，但我并不介意自己打扫房间。而且我希望能够装饰自己的房间。

汤姆： 这是个很好的理由。那你就一定要找间公寓了。

小丫： 问题是我对公寓的位置和价格一点也不了解。

汤姆： 这不是问题。别担心，我们总会解决的。实在不行我们还可以谷歌搜索啊。

小丫： 我们在中国有和谷歌一样的搜索引擎，叫百度，但是我们叫"度娘"，意思就是杜女士。比起谷歌，大多数中国人还是喜欢用百度。

汤姆： 我听说了，但是在这儿百度不是很受欢迎。

小丫： 你住在哪儿？我从来没问过你和杰瑞住在哪儿。在学校附近吗？

汤姆： 还是有点远的，我是说大概要走15分钟吧。

小丫： 15分钟还算远？在中国的时候，我每天都要走15分钟以上才能到学校。

汤姆： 好呀，所以你是完全有准备的喽。

小丫： 当然啦。我们现在要开始着手细节吧。

会话2

Tom: What's your budget for the apartment? From the information I got from the internet, the prices for an apartment with one room vary between $450 dollar to $800 dollar.

Ya: It's much more expensive than I thought. How does the 450 room look?

Tom: Take a look at the picture here. It's not bad. There's a shower, a small kitchen, and some closets. Have you ever thought about sharing a house or an apartment with a roommate, like Jerry and me?

Ya: I guess I can do that, too. What about the price?

Tom: It's cheaper than the apartment, but you will share the kitchen and the bathroom. Is that fine for you?

Ya: That's perfectly fine for me. We even share one room with other students in China. I used to live with three other girls in high school.

Tom: Ok. Then we have more choices. This room looks good. It's in a house with three floors, and your room will be on the second floor. There's a girl living on the same floor. Two other girls live on the top floor. It looks like a girls' student house.

Ya: That sounds interesting. I don't really want to share a house with boys I don't know. How is the location and the price?

Tom: It's less than 10 minutes' walk from school. The rent is 250 per month. Sounds good to me! Plus you've got a balcony as well.

Ya: It looks nice. Is any furniture in the room?

Tom: Let's see. It has a bed, a desk, a bookshelf and a wardrobe, and nice curtains.

Ya: I'm highly interested now. Shall we go to take a look?

Tom: Why not? Let's go there.

汤姆： 你对公寓的预算是多少？从我在网上看到的信息来看，一间卧室的公寓价格在450美元和800美元之间。

小丫： 比我预想的贵多了。450美元的公寓看起来怎么样？

汤姆： 来看看这张照片，还不错。有淋浴，一个小厨房，还有一些柜子。你考虑过跟室友同住一栋房子或者一间公寓吗，像我和杰瑞这样？

小丫： 我想我也可以。价钱怎么样？

汤姆： 比自己租公寓便宜，不过要和室友共用厨房和卫生间。这样你可以接受吗？

小丫： 完全没问题。在中国，我们甚至和别的学生住同一间寝室。我高中的时候，就和另外三个女生住一间寝室。

汤姆： 这样啊。那我们就有更多的选择了。这间卧室看起来不错，它在一栋三层的房子里面的二楼。有一个女孩也住在二楼。另外还有两个女孩住顶楼。看来这是一个女生的学生公寓。

小丫： 听起来不错。我不太喜欢跟不认识的男生合住。位置和价钱怎么样？

汤姆： 步行去学校的话要10分钟。租金是每月250美元。听起来不错。而且你还有个阳台呢！

小丫： 看起来是不错。房间里有什么家具呢？

汤姆： 让我们看看。有床、桌子、书架、衣柜，另外窗帘真好看。

小丫： 我非常有兴趣！我们可以去看一看吗？

汤姆： 为什么不呢？我们现在就去。

必备词汇

curtain
['kə:tən] n.

窗帘，门帘，幕布

冷战时期，东欧国家和西欧国家之间的铁幕称作"the iron curtain"。

例如 She likes to keep the curtain open in the day, so the sun can shine through the window. 她喜欢白天把窗帘打开，这样阳光可以通过窗户照进来。

balcony
['bælkəni] n.

阳台，露台，晒台

例如 Her parents keep many flowers in the balcony. 她父母在阳台养了很多花。

closet
['klɔzit] n.

壁橱，衣柜，柜子

虽然有衣柜之意，但并不特指衣柜，意义比较宽泛。

例如 He hangs the coats of the guests in the closet. 他把客人的衣服挂在壁橱里。

freedom
['fri:dəm] n.

自由，自由度，解脱

形容词形式是free，意为自由的，免费的。**例如** Generations and generations have been fighting for freedom. 几代人都在为自由而战。

location
[ləu'keiʃən] n.

位置，定位，地点

例如 This shop's location is one of the reasons for its success. 这家店的位置是其成功的原因之一。

pretty
['priti] adv.

很，相当

和大家熟知的adj. 漂亮，好看的词性和词义都有很大差别。**例如** He looks pretty young in that T-shirt. 他穿那件T恤看起来很年轻。

decorate
['dekəreit] v.

装饰，装点，装潢

名词形式为decoration，不可数名词。**例如** One of the greatest fun at Christmas is to decorate the Christmas tree. 圣诞节最大的快乐之一就是装饰圣诞树。They are planning on the decoration of the baby room. 他们在计划宝宝房的装饰。

apartment
[ə'pɑ:tmənt] n.

公寓房间，公寓大楼

我们一般人的住房并不是大家所说的house，而是apartment，我们的居民楼也就是apartment building。**例如** Their apartment is in the city center. 他们的公寓在市中心。

feed
[fi:d] v.

喂养，饲养

但本课中出现的be fed up (with sth)是feed的变形。**例如** They feed the horses with corn. 他们用玉米来喂养马。After three weeks of working over time, I'm fed up with my current job. 在连续加班三个星期后，我真是厌倦了现在的工作。

vary
['vεəri] v.

变化，变更

形容词形式various，意为"多变的，变化的，多种的"。**例如** The color of this paint varies with the temperature. 这种油漆的颜色随着温度改变而改变。

wardrobe
['wɔ:drəub] n.

衣柜，衣橱

对比上面的closet，意思更集中在衣柜，而不是一般的柜子。**例如** There is always a wardrobe in the bedroom. 卧室里通常有一个衣柜。

地道美语

① Back in China... 在中国的时候……注意句中back的用法，意为曾经在某地的时候，多用于和现在做对比。例如：

A: Back in the States, we always had problems with the traffic.
B: It's not much better here in Japan.

A: 原来在美国的时候，我们的交通很成问题。
B: 日本也没比美国好很多。

2 I don't really mind cleaning the room. 我不是很介意打扫房间。注意句中mind doing sth的用法，是美语口语中的常用表达，意为"介意做某事，不喜欢做某事"。例如：

A: Isn't it too far to walk to school every day?

B: I don't really mind. I always have music with me.

　A：每天走路上学不是很远吗？

　B：我其实不是很介意，我总是听音乐。

3 I mean it's like 15 minutes on foot. 我是说走路大概需要15分钟。注意句中I mean...的用法，类似于汉语的"就是说，所以说"，是美语中常见的口头禅。例如：

A: It's complicated. I mean, you put it on and then take it off after a certain while.

B: Yeah, I see what you mean.

　A：这很复杂。我是说，你要先穿上，然后过一会儿再脱下来。

　B：是的，我明白你的意思了。

4 I'm fed up with my hostel room. 我住够了青年旅社的房间。注意句中的be fed up with sth的使用，是美语常用表达方式，意为"对……感到厌烦，腻了"。例如：

A: I'm fed up with eating pasta every day. Let's try something new this evening.

B: All right. It's up to you.

　A：每天吃意大利面我已经吃腻了。今天晚上我们吃点新鲜的吧。

　B：没问题呀。你说了算。

⑤ I've heard of it. 我听说过。注意句中hear of的用法，意为"听说"；有时hear单独使用，同样表示听说。例如：

A: A house on the beach costs 6 million dollars. It's too expensive for me.

B: Are you sure? That's not what I heard.

A：一栋在海边的房子要600万美元。对我来说太贵了。

B：你确定吗？这可跟我听说的不一样。

⑥ Skeleton in the closet. 家丑。中国有句古话"家丑不可外扬"，家丑意指不愿被外人知道的事情。例如：

A: Her mom has been a drug addict for years, but she hasn't told anyone about this.

B: Every family has a skeleton in the closet. I hope she's fine.

A：她妈妈已经吸毒好多年了，但是她从来没跟别人说起过这件事。

B：家家都有不可告人的秘密。我希望她过得还好。

⑦ That's a fair reason. 这是个合理的理由。句中的fair跟大家熟知的"公正，公平"之意略有差别，意为"合理并可以接受的"。例如：

A: I can't go at 8 o'clock, because I have to take my brother to school first. It's important.

B: Ok, that's fair enough. We can change it to 8:40.

A：我不能8点去，因为我要先送弟弟上学。这很重要。

B：好吧，合情合理，那我们改到8:40。

8 **We can sort it out. 我们会想出办法的。注意句中sort out 的用法，意为"解决，处理"。例如：**

A: I have so many documents to read, but I don't have much time left before the deadline.

B: Don't worry. We will sort things out.

A：我要读这么多资料，但是在最后期限之前我没有 那么多时间了。

B：别担心。我们会想出办法解决的。

表达方式百宝箱

本课我们学习了关于房子及居住方面的一些词汇，同学 们要整理复习，那么我们就在下面一起整理一下地道的表达 方式吧！

Every family has a skeleton in the closet. 家家都有不可告 人的秘密。

I don't really mind cleaning the room. 我不是很介意打扫房间。

I mean it's like 15 minutes on foot. 我是说走路大概需要15 分钟。

I'm fed up with my hostel room. 我住够了青年旅社的房间。

I've heard of it. 我听说过。

We can sort it out. 我们会想出办法的。

You are all prepared. 你是都准备好了。

小丫 带你走遍美国

住宿

舒适开心的住宿生活能够保障学生顺利完成学业。相反，住宿的不适也会影响到学生的生活，因此，选对适合学生的住宿方式至关重要。国际学生在美国有三种住宿选择：学生宿舍、寄宿家庭以及自己租房。这三种寄宿方式各有利弊。其中寄宿家庭我们已经在前面了解过了，这里主要了解一下其他两种住宿方式。

学生宿舍，平时上下课非常方便。课后参加课外活动，获取图书馆自修等也不用考虑路程和时间问题。同时，还能使用到学校诸如餐厅、体育馆、健身房、俱乐部、游泳池等公共设施。另外，美国很多学校的学生宿舍内提供免费有线电视、上网服务、市内电话服务、邮件传送/电报服务，这也大大方便了学生的生活。另外，基本每个宿舍都有宿舍管理员，校园里也会有专门的保安进行巡查。同时放学后学生也不用离开校园，安全方面可以说是最有保障的。但缺点在于要和其他几名学生同住一间宿舍，生活方式和文化背景的不同可能有时会造成不愉快。

自己租房这种住宿方式一般适合在美国待过一段时间，并对当地的生活有所了解的学生。通常学生都会选择合租方式。三五个好友一起租个房子，然后平摊房费。租房的好处在于学生比较自由，通常学生也会在学校附近租，出入学校也比较方便。但在租房时需要考虑到的问题还不少呢，包括交通、治安、是否有家具、是否要有室友等等。

我们的小丫选择自己租房是独立的开始，让我们为她加油吧！

第8课

周末派对: 场合与主题

情景介绍 小丫从小到大也参加过不少同学的生日会，或者节假日和三五个好友一起出游，但到美国以后还没参加过真正美国年轻人的聚会呢。恰巧，机会来了，杰西卡的好朋友艾玛过生日，邀请大家一起来庆祝。

会话1

Jerry: Good morning! Is Ya there?

Ya: Hi, Jerry. This is me. What's up?

Jerry: I have some fun news for you. Jessica's friend Emma is throwing a party for her birthday, and she invited us all.

Ya: I don't know Emma, and she doesn't know me either.

Jerry: I know that, but she invited Tom, and Tom has to bring a girl, so that must be you. Oh, maybe I should have told Tom before you. It doesn't matter. Are you free next Saturday?

Ya: I think so.

Jerry: Then you are in?

Ya: Absolutely.

Jerry: Great! You can talk with Tom about the theme. I gotta go. See you.

Ya: All right. See you.

(Calling Tom)

Tom: Yeah? Jerry already told you about Emma's party. You know, if you don't have time, you don't have to come. I can go alone.

Ya: Of course I want to go. It will be the first time that I've been to a real American party. It means something to me.

Tom: Then we probably should talk about the theme of that party.

Ya: Interesting. I've never been to a theme party.

Tom: Well, Emma likes *Gossip Girls*, and she wants her party to be exactly the same, which means we need to dress up like the characters.

Ya: I also watched *Gossip Girls* back in China. Let me guess. Emma will be Queen B.

Tom: I have no idea who Queen B is, but yes, you are right.

Ya: I'm curious about this party. I've seen pool parties in movies, which look wild and crazy to me. Happily this isn't like that.

Tom: Pool parties are quite normal to me, at least acceptable. This TV series theme is a bit beyond my imagination.

Ya: I have an idea! We can pretend to be two new students, so that we won't need to dress ourselves up like anyone in the soap.

Tom: It's indeed a good idea. We will also avoid the problem of being the same with someone else at the party. I can't wait to see how Jerry and Jessica will do this.

杰瑞：	早上好！小丫在吗？
小丫：	嗨，杰瑞！我就是小丫。什么事？
杰瑞：	我有好玩的事情要告诉你。杰西卡的朋友艾玛要办一个生日晚会，她邀请了我们大家参加。
小丫：	我和艾玛互不认识啊。
杰瑞：	这个我知道。但是她邀请了汤姆，他一定要带个女伴儿去吧，那就一定是你了。哦，或许我应该先告诉汤姆。没关系啦。你下周六晚上有空吗？
小丫：	我觉得有空。
杰瑞：	来参加吧？
小丫：	当然啦。

杰瑞： 太好了，关于晚会的主题你可以跟汤姆聊。我要先挂了，下次见哦。

小丫： 好吧，下次见。

（打电话给汤姆）

汤姆： 喂？杰瑞已经把艾玛的晚会告诉你了吧。你知道的，如果你下周六没有时间，可以不用来的，我可以自己去。

小丫： 我当然想去了。这将是我第一次参加真正的美国晚会，对我很有意义呢。

汤姆： 那我们就该谈谈晚会的主题了。

小丫： 有意思。我还从来没去过主题派对呢。

汤姆： 嗯，艾玛喜欢《绯闻女孩》，所以她想让这场派对跟电视剧一模一样，也就是说我们要打扮得像剧中的人物。

小丫： 我以前在中国的时候也看《绯闻女孩》。让我猜猜，艾玛想做布莱尔女王吗？

汤姆： 我一点也不知道你说的布莱尔女王是谁，但是你却说对了。

小丫： 我对这场派对很好奇。以前在电影里看过游泳池派对，觉得既狂野又疯狂，还好我们不是那样的派对。

汤姆： 游泳池派对对我来说倒是很正常的，起码可以接受。这场电视连续剧派对却是有点超乎我的想象。

小丫： 我有个主意！我们可以假装成两个新学生，然后我们就不用把自己打扮成电视剧里的任何人物了。

汤姆： 这确实是个好主意。我们还可以避免装扮成跟别人一样的人物。我已经迫不及待想看看杰瑞和杰西卡怎么打扮了。

必备词汇

throw
[θrəu] v.

举办，常见用法为throw a party

这和大家熟知的"扔，掷"意思很不相同。**例如** The Smiths throw a grand Christmas party every year. 史密斯一家每年圣诞节都会举办一场盛大的圣诞晚会。

gossip
['gɔsip] v.

说闲话，说长道短

n. 流言蜚语，闲话，绯闻。**例如** Julie likes to gossip about the affair of her neighbors. 朱莉喜欢传她邻居们的绯闻。The gossip between Lily and Peter is all around. 莉莉和彼得的绯闻传得满天飞。

avoid
[ə'vɔid] v.

避免，避开，躲开

宾语可以是sb., sth.或者doing sth.。**例如** I avoid him as much as possible. 我尽量避开他。With all the luck, he avoided an accident. 真是足够幸运，他避免了一场车祸。They avoid mentioning the name of their lost child. 他们避免提及去世孩子的名字。

soap
[səup] n.

（口语）肥皂剧，和大家熟知的"肥皂"可不是一个意思。

本课中用于表示没有深刻主题的电视连续剧。

curious
['kjuəriəs] adj.

好奇的，渴望知道的，爱探求的

配合about sth.或者to do sth.使用。

例如 The boy is curious about the animals. 这个男孩对动物感到好奇。The student is curious to hear what the professor is going to say about his report. 这个学生对教授即将对他的报告发表的评价很好奇。

absolutely
['æbsəlu:tli, æbsə'lu:tli] adv.

绝对地，完全地；（口语用于对答）一点不错，完全对

本课出现的正是口语中常见的意思。

theme
[θi:m] n.

主题，题材

本课中出现的theme party意为主题派对，前几课学过theme park意为主题公园。

wild
[waild] adj.

狂野的，无法无天的

wild animal意为野生动物，但是wild party就意为狂野的派对。

beyond
[bi'jɔnd] prep.

超出，超越于……之外

例如 The benefits of reading goes beyond this. 阅读带来的好处还不止于此。

happily
['hæpili] adv.

幸运地，幸好

例如 Happily, nobody got hurt in the accident. 幸运的是没有人在这场事故中受伤。

acceptable [ək'septəbl] adj.

正常的，可以忍受的，值得接受的

例如 This is not his best work, but it's still acceptable. 这不是他的最佳作品，但还是可以接受的。

normal ['nɔːməl] adj.

正常的，正规的，标准的

我们常说的普通人便是normal people。副词形式是normally，意为"一般情况下，正常情况下"。**例如** Normally, we take a shower before entering the swimming pool. 正常情况下，我们进入游泳池之前先冲个澡。

地道美语

1 Are you free next Saturday? 你下周六有时间吗？比起Do you have time next Saturday? 这种说法更加简洁，也更加适合年轻人。例如：

A: Laura, are you free tomorrow? I need some advice on my summer trip.

B: Sure. I'll see you tomorrow at 10 o'clock.

A：劳拉，你明天有时间吗？我需要点关于暑假旅行的建议。

B：没问题，我们明天上午10点见。

2 I can't wait to see... 我迫不及待想看/知道……表示想知道某事结果的强烈欲望。例如：

A: My dad bought a new race car. It's so cool.

B: Really? I can't wait to see it.

　　A: 我爸爸买了辆新跑车。它太酷了。

　　B: 真的吗？我迫不及待想看看。

例句中出现的race car意为跑车，同义说法还有sports car。

---

③ I gotta go. 我得走了。可以表示要去一个地方，即字面意义上的离开，也可以表示要去做别的事情。例如：

A: I gotta go. The train will start in 10 minutes.

B: Sure. Have a nice journey.

　　A: 我得走了，还有10分钟火车就开车了。

　　B: 当然。旅途愉快。

---

④ It means something to me. 这对我有一定意义。相反地，It doesn't mean anything to me. 对我来说这毫无意义。例如：

A: Look at this dress. It means a lot to me. It was the dress I was wearing the night David proposed.

B: So sweet. I can imagine what it means to you.

　　A: 看这条裙子。它对我意义非凡。这是大卫求婚那晚我穿的裙子。

　　B: 真温馨。我可以想象它对你的意义。

---

⑤ Jessica's friend Emma is throwing a party for her birthday. 杰西卡的朋友艾玛要办一个生日派对。句中的throw a party为地道的美语表达，对比hold a party生动很多。例如：

A: It's a lot of work to throw a party, the catering and the cleaning.

B: But if all the people enjoy it, everything is worth it.

A：举办派对是很大的工作量。要提供餐饮，还要打扫。

B：但是如果大家都喜欢，那一切都值得。

句中的catering 意为"承办酒席，提供餐饮服务"。caterer专指宴会/酒席承办人。

6 **Let me guess、让我猜猜。和前几课中学过的let me see、结构相同。例如：**

A: How much do you think this watch cost?

B: Let me guess. It looks expensive.

A：你觉得这块表多少钱？

B：让我猜猜。它看起来很贵啊。

7 **Oh, maybe I should have...、哦，或许我应该……这是一种虚拟式的口语表达方法，表示对过去未做某事的遗憾。例如：**

A: Your car looks a bit used.

B: Maybe I should have washed it yesterday. It looks much better when it's clean.

A：你的车看起来有点旧。

B：或许我昨天应该去洗车。它干净的时候看起来好很多。

8 **What's up? 什么事？/怎么了？是美国年轻人常用的口语表达方式。朋友见面时也可以问what's up?意为最近怎么样。**

例如：

A: Hey, Tony, what's up?

B: Nothing new, but not bad. And you?

A: 嗨，托尼。最近怎么样？

B: 没什么新鲜事，但还不错。你呢？

9 You know... 你知道吗？／你知道的……美语中常见的口头禅，并不是在向对方提问，也不期待对方回答。例如：

A: Sometimes I don't know what he wants. You know, it's hard to fully understand a person.

B: I know. I have the same feeling.

A: 有时我不知道他想要什么。你知道的，想要完全理解一个人很难。

B: 我知道。我也有同感。

表达方式百宝箱

本课中小丫分别在电话上和杰瑞还有汤姆谈论了周末主题派对的事，出现了一些美国年轻人常用的口语表达方式，现在就让我们一起来总结一下吧！

What's up? 什么事？／最近怎么样？

I gotta go. 我得走了。

Are you free next Saturday? 你下周六有时间吗？

Oh, maybe I should have... 哦，或许我应该……

It means something to me. 它对我很有意义。／它对我有一定的意义。

You know... 你知道吗？/你知道的……
It doesn't matter. 没关系。/无所谓。
I can't wait to see... 我迫不及待想看/知道……
It's indeed a good idea. 这的确是个好主意。

小丫 带你走遍美国

《绯闻女孩》(Gossip Girl)——美国热播青春偶像剧

　　《绯闻女孩》（英语：Gossip Girl）是由Cecily von Ziegesar所写的系列小说改编的美国青春偶像剧，所讲述的是曼哈顿上层社会阶层，纽约一个私立学校里面富豪子弟的生活面貌。其中的Gossip Girl是曼哈顿上东区最神秘的人物，她是了解上层社会贵族巨细无遗的生活的唯一来源，而且拥有一众随时随地为她提供八卦消息的公子哥和千金女。

　　这部电视剧是第一部将现在时髦而流行的"博客"、"手机短信"这些元素当做核心主题，但是又不让人感到做作、生硬、虚假和故弄玄虚的电视剧。而且不仅有养眼的美女帅哥，有高潮起伏的精彩剧情，更有令人眼花缭乱的时尚造型。剧中的主要流行元素有：发带、各种颜色质地的袜子、搭配完美的校园风、坏男孩Chuck的立领，当然少不了女孩子装饰发型的贝雷帽。

　　在剧中，常可以听到"xoxo"，表示"hugs and kisses"，"x"代表一个吻，特别是在信件署名处。"xoxo"被现代人用来表示信件署名时的"亲吻拥抱"。我们的小丫对剧情很了解，相信她会在派对中过得很愉快。

第9课

出行：地铁和巴士

情景介绍：不论是在国内还是在国外，使用公共交通工具出行一直是备受欢迎的方式，方便快捷而且价格低廉。今天就让我们来看看小丫是怎么在纽约乘坐地铁和巴士的吧。

会话1

Ya: What's the best way to go to Manhattan? Is it the center of New York?

Tom: We can say it's the financial and business center of New York. Wall street lies on the south end, with banks and stock exchanges on the sides. The United Nations Buildings are also in that area. There you can find Broadway, the Empire State Building and the central park.

Ya: This is exactly why I want to go there. There are so many things that I've been dreaming to see. How can we get there?

Tom: The best way will be with the subway. It's fast and most importantly, underground.

Ya: We have subways in many cities in China, but I don't know if it works the same way in the States. Generally the same I guess.

Tom: I've never been to China, so I don't know how Chinese subways work. You will see in the station.

(In the subway station)

Tom: We can buy the tickets either with the ticket vendor or from the ticket box.

Ya: I want to give the ticket vendor a try. All right, here we are, and destination Manhattan. Yes! 2 dollars, not very much.

Tom: Find any difference so far?

Ya: Not yet. There's no hurry. I'm not here to be picky.

Tom: Take it easy, Ya. Nobody is saying anything here.

Ya: I'm cool, so don't worry. Aha, there is difference Number One, no scanner.

Tom: Scanner? For what?

Ya: In China, before you get on the subway, you need to have you stuff scanned, to see nothing harmful gets to the subway.

小丫： 去曼哈顿的最好办法是什么？它是纽约的市中心吗？

汤姆： 我们可以说它是纽约的金融和商业中心。华尔街就坐落在曼哈顿南段，满是银行和证券交易所。联合国大楼也在曼哈顿，另外在那还有百老汇、帝国大厦和中央公园。

小丫： 这正是我想去那儿的原因，那里有很多东西都是我一直梦想见到的。我们怎么才能去曼哈顿呢？

汤姆： 最好的办法应该是坐地铁，速度快。而且最重要的是它走地下。

小丫： 在中国我们很多城市有地铁，但是我不知道这儿的地铁是不是一样。不过我猜大体上应该一样吧。

汤姆： 我没去过中国，所以不知道中国的地铁什么样。到地铁站你就知道了。

（在地铁站）

汤姆： 我们可以在自动售票机买票，也可以去售票处买票。

小丫： 我想试试自动售票机。好的，我们在这儿，终点是曼哈顿。成了！2美元，不是很贵。

汤姆： 到现在为止发现什么区别了吗？

小丫： 还没有。不着急。我又不是来挑刺的。

汤姆： 别紧张啊，小丫，谁也没说什么。

小丫： 我很好啊，别担心。啊哈！看到第一个区别了，纽约没有安检扫描！

汤姆： 扫描？什么扫描？

小丫： 在中国，乘坐地铁之前要扫描随身物品，以检查有没有有害物品被带上地铁。

必备词汇

Broadway
['brɔːdwei] n.
百老汇；代指纽约的戏剧界
例如 Her dream is to play in Broadway.
她的梦想是在百老汇演出。

empire
['empaiə] n.
帝国，大企业，君权，皇权
empirer n. 君主，皇帝

financial
[fai'nænʃəl] adj.
财政的，金融的；名词形式为finance
例如 New York is one of the most important financial centers of the world.
纽约是世界最重要的金融中心之一。

generally
['dʒenərəli] adv.
通常地，一般地，普遍地；形容词形式为general
例如 Generally speaking, you did a very good job. 总体来说，你们做得非常好。

harmful
['hɑːmful] adj.
有害的，能造成损失的
例如 What he did was very harmful for the reputation of our company. 他的行为对公司的名誉非常不利。

vendor
['vendə:] n.

小贩，叫卖者，自动售货机

我们平时买饮料或者小零食的自动售货机也称为vending machine。

scanner
['skænə] n.

扫描仪，扫描设备；动词形式为scan，意为扫描，细看，审视

例如 There's a luggage scanner in the subway station. 在地铁站有一个行李扫描器。

stock exchange
[iks'tʃeindʒ]

证券交易所

例如 He got some inside news from his friend who works in the stock exchange. 他从一个在证券交易所工作的朋友那里得到了一些内部消息。

underground
['ʌndəgraund] adj.

地下的，地面下的；秘密的，不公开的

例如 An underground passage leads to the parking lot. 一条地下通道通到停车场。They are suspected of underground business. 他们被怀疑从事秘密交易。

地道美语

① Find any difference so far? 到现在为止找到什么区别了吗？
句中有两点需要注意：1、口语中经常把提问的助动词省

略；2. so far意为"到目前为止"，常见词组so far so good意为"到目前为止一切顺利"。例如：

A: Hear any good news?

B: Not yet, but I'm still hoping.

A: 听到什么好消息了吗？

B: 还没有，但是我还抱着希望。

② **Here we are** 我们在这儿。/我们说到这儿了。用于日常对话中，不一定表示在某一个位置，也可以表示谈话进行的进度。例如：

A: All right. Here we are. Last time we discussed the details concerning the decoration of the new house.

B: I already made a proposal. Please take a look.

A: 好的，我们说到这了。上次我们讨论了新房子装修的细节。

B: 我已经做了一个提案，请您看一下。

③ **I want to give the ticket vendor a try.** 我想试一试自动售票机。句中两点需要注意：1. ticket vendor意为"自动售票机"，或者ticket vending machine；2. give sth a try意为"给……一个机会，尝试……"。例如：

A: I don't want to take the airplane. It's not safe.

B: Of course it's safe. Trust me, give it a try.

A: 我不想坐飞机。不安全。

B: 飞机当然安全啦。相信我，试试吧。

4 **I'm cool.** 我很好。cool with sth意为"与……相安无事，很好"。并不是"我很酷，或者我很凉爽"的意思。例如：

A: I'm cool with Jenny now. We are still working in one team.

B: That's good to know.

A：我现在和珍妮相处得很好，我们仍在同一个小组工作。

B：这是个好消息。

---

5 **So picky** 真挑剔。是有点不礼貌的说法，意在表明对方或者被提及者挑剔，不易相处。例如：

A: Has he always been so picky?

B: Yes, he doesn't like to talk.

A：他一直这么挑剔吗？

B：是啊，他不喜欢与人交谈。

---

6 **Take it easy.** 别着急，别紧张。是在对方紧张，焦虑或者生气时缓和气氛的用语。例如：

A: What do you mean? What were you saying?

B: Take it easy. I was just trying to share an opinion.

A：你什么意思？你刚才说什么？

B：别紧张，我只是想分享一下自己的观点。

7 There's no hurry./ No hurry. 不着急。区别于"Take it easy"，这里指不需要赶时间，类似于"慢慢来"的意思。例如：

A: When do I need to finish this task?

B: There's no hurry. I want you to take your time.

　　A：我需要什么时候完成这项任务？

　　B：不着急，我想让你慢慢完成。

8 This is exactly why... 这正是……的原因。美式口语中常出现exactly，意为"正是……"，例如：

A: I was stuck in the traffic jam for more than one hour this morning.

B: This is exactly why I take the subway to work.

　　A：今天早晨我堵车堵了一个小时。

　　B：这正是我坐地铁上班的原因。

句中的be stuck意为"卡住"，例如：The ball is stuck in the bottle neck. 球卡在瓶颈处了。

9 You need to have you stuff scanned. 你需要扫描检查随身物品。

注意句中have/ get sth done的用法，意为"让/叫/使某人做某事"。例如：

A: I need to get my hair done for the coming summer.

B: I know a good hair dresser.

A：夏天就快到了，我要去做头发。

B：我知道一家很好的理发店。

表达方式百宝箱

Find any difference so far? 到现在为止找到什么区别了吗?

Here we are. 我们在这。我们说到这了。

I want to give the ticket vendor a try. 我想试试自动售票机。

I'm cool. 我很好。

Nobody is saying anything here. 谁也没说什么呀。

Take it easy. 别着急。别紧张。

There's no hurry. 不着急。

This is exactly why... 这正是……的原因。

小丫带你走遍美国

纽约地铁

纽约市于1868年首次建成高架铁路并投入客运，后因噪音及污染严重，除保留少量郊区线路作为以后兴建地铁的延伸线外，已陆续予以拆除。第一条建于地下的地铁于1907年建成通车，总长443.74米，设车站504个，居世界首位。其中地上线路约占44%，绝大部分为高架线。地下部分除过河段等少数区段用盾构法施工外，绝大部分均用明挖法施工。地铁轨距1435毫米，分别以600伏、625伏和650伏直流3轨供电。纽约地铁的特点是24小时运营，有些运量较大的线路，还采用3条或4条轨道，实现了快慢车分道行驶！是世界上最著名的十大地铁。

经过一个多世纪的发展，纽约市地铁仍旧是号称全世界最有效率的地铁系统。纽约市目前拥有地铁线路26条，地铁站468个，车厢6400多节，线路总长近370公里，每天载运450万人来往纽约5大区。据统计，在每天进入曼哈顿中央商务区的客流中，搭乘地铁到达的为62.8%。哥伦比亚大学研究纽约历史的学者凯斯·杰克逊认为，如果没有地铁，每天都会有更多车辆进入曼哈顿，交通堵塞和昂贵的停车费将使纽约市无法居住，纽约不可能成为像现在这样伟大的城市。

在倡导环保和推崇公共交通工具的今天，纽约地铁的高效率运转也给我们很大的启发，搭乘地铁让小丫更加了解纽约的历史和文化了。

第10课

超市购物

情景介绍： 很多来美国的留学生对去超市购物都有恐惧心理，不仅是因为语言上的障碍，更加因为饮食习惯上的差异。进入超市不知道该买些什么，也不知道同种商品的不同类型之间有何差异，我们的小丫也遇到了同样的问题。今天，我们就来看一下小丫是怎么解决这个问题的吧……

会话1

Tom: Ya, I'm going to the supermarket this afternoon. Do you want to come along?

Ya: Sure! I get confused all the time about what to buy.

Tom: Americans like to take a shopping list with them when they shop in the supermarket.

(In the supermarket)

Ya: I feel like some beer. Where is the beer?

Tom: They don't have beer in this supermarket. We have to go to the liquor store.

Ya: Seriously? They don't have beer. How can that be?

Tom: It's the state law. Alcohol is not allowed to be sold in supermarkets in some states of America, only in liquor stores.

Ya: This is very strict.

Tom: Yes, I agree, but this is the rule.

Ya: Do they sell organic vegetables here?

Tom: Yes, they do. They're right in front of you. The organic vegetables ate marked with the blue label. Here on the packet. Do you see it?

Ya: Oh, yes. They use a special sign, so people could identify which are organic and which aren't. Do you know where the soy sauce is?

Tom: I think that will be in aisle 6, with the condiments. It's right next to the ketchup.

Ya: Shopping with you is so easy.

汤姆： 小丫，我今天下午去超市，你要一起去吗？

小丫： 当然了！我总是不知道要买什么？

汤姆： 美国人去超市购物时喜欢随身带一个购物清单。

（在超市里）

小丫： 我想买点啤酒。啤酒在哪里？

汤姆： 超市里不卖啤酒，我们要去酒类饮料商店才行。

小丫： 真的吗？他们没有啤酒？怎么会这样呢？

汤姆： 这是州法，在美国的一些州，酒类饮料不允许在超市出售，只能在酒类饮料商店购买。

小丫： 这很严格啊。

汤姆： 是啊，我同意，但这就是规定。

小丫： 这有有机蔬菜吗？

汤姆： 他们有有机蔬菜。有机蔬菜就在前面，是蓝色标签的。在这儿，在包装袋上。看见了吗？

小丫： 哦，这样啊，看见了。他们用特殊标签标出来，所以人们就能区分有机蔬菜和非有机蔬菜了。你知道酱油在哪儿吗？

汤姆： 我觉得应该在第六排，调味品区，就在番茄酱旁边。

小丫： 跟你一起购物真容易。

会话2

Ya: We are having more and more supermarkets in China. With the improvement of people's living standards, supermarkets are springing up like mushrooms.

Tom: I can imagine. It's easy to shop in the supermarket. What you need to do is to walk your handcart along the aisles and take anything you need from the shelves to fill your cart.

Ya: Exactly. In the supermarket, we can find food, clothes, drinks, books and many other things in your arm's reach.

Tom: Don't forget that sometimes you buy one and get one for free!

Ya: Of course. I like discounts, but most of the time the price is fixed in the supermarket.

Tom: Actually most of the shops in the States only offer fixed prices.

Ya: I forgot I also need to buy butter and cheese.

Tom: Cool. You already start trying butter and cheese. Which cheese do you like?

Ya: I hear cheese tastes like smelly socks. Is it true?

Tom: Well, I can only say people who say these are not used to the taste or smell of cheese. You can start with young cheese. The taste is softer than old cheese.

Ya: Ok. Which is young cheese then?

Tom: Try Philadelphia. I think you will like it. If you don't, I can take over...

> **小丫：** 在中国，超市数量越来越多。随着人们生活水平的提高，超市像雨后春笋般涌现出来。

> **汤姆：** 我可以想象。在超市购物很方便。你只需要推着手推车在货架间行走，然后把你需要的东西从货架上拿下来放到购物车里就可以了。

> **小丫：** 说的正是。在超市里，我们可以买到食物、衣服、饮料、书籍和很多其他的东西，都是伸手就拿得到的。

> **汤姆：** 别忘了，有时是买一赠一！

> **小丫：** 当然不会忘啦。我喜欢买有折扣的东西，但是大部分时候超市里的物价都是固定的。

> **汤姆：** 其实在美国的大部分商店都只有固定价格。

> **小丫：** 我差点忘了，我还要买……

> **汤姆：** 不错啊。你已经开始尝试黄油和奶酪了。你喜欢什么奶酪呢？

> **小丫：** 我听说奶酪的味道像臭袜子。这是真的吗？

> **汤姆：** 嗯，我只能说，说这话的人还不适应奶酪的味道。你可以先尝试发酵时间比较短的奶酪，它们的味道比发酵时间长的奶酪的味道要柔和一些。

> **小丫：** 好的，哪些奶酪是发酵时间短的奶酪呢？

> **汤姆：** 试试卡夫菲力奶油芝士吧。我觉得你会喜欢的。如果你不喜欢，可以给我……

必备词汇

condiment
['kɔndimənt] n.

调料，调味品

日常生活中的油盐酱醋都统称为 condiment。

例如 Soy sauce is a normal condiment in China. 在中国酱油是种很普通的调料。

confused
[kən'fju:zd] adj.

困惑的，烦恼的，迷惑的

注意区分confusing adj. 令人困惑的，令人烦恼的。动词形式为confuse v. 使困惑，使糊涂，使混淆。

例如 He's still confused about what happened. 他对刚发生的事还是很疑惑。

cheese
[tʃi:z] n.

乳酪，干酪，芝士

是一种用奶放酸之后增加酶或细菌制作的食品。大多奶酪呈乳白色或金黄色。

例如 France is famous for its cheese. 法国以其乳酪著名。

packet
['pækit] n.

小包裹，小袋，包装

例如 In the supermarket, you can buy tea in small packets. 在超市可以买到小包装的茶。

label
['leibl] n.

商标，标签

例如 The washing instructions are written on the label. 洗涤说明印在标签上。

mark
[mɑːk] v.

标记，做记号

同时名词形式mark n. 标记，记号。

例如 There is a red mark on the door. 门上有个红色的标记。

living standard
['stændəd]

生活水平，生活标准

例如 The current living standard is much higher than twenty years ago. 现在的生活水平比20年前高很多。

organic
[ɔː'gænik] adj.

有机的，有机体的，生物的

我们在超市中常见的"有机蔬菜"是organic vegetables。

liquor
['likə] n.

酒，含酒精饮料；在美国尤指烈酒

例如 Alcohol can only be found in liquor stores in some States. 在一些州只有在酒品专卖店才能买到酒。

shelf
[ʃelf] n.

架子，隔板，货架

例如 There is a big book shelf in his room. 在他的房间里有一个大书架。

butter
['bʌtə] n.

黄油，牛油

是一种奶制品，把新鲜牛奶加以搅拌之后再把上层的浓稠状物体滤去部分水分，剩下的就是黄油。在西方国家是必不可少的调味品，但脂肪含量偏高。

例如 He likes to eat bread with butter. 他喜欢把面包和黄油一起吃。

soy sauce
[sɔɪə] [sɔːs] n.

酱油

aisle
[ail] n.

过道，通道

列车、飞机中的过道都称为aisle。本课中特指超市货架之间的过道。**例如** I like to sit next to the aisle instead of the window in the airplane. 在飞机上，比起靠窗的座位，我更喜欢坐在过道旁边。

ketchup
['ketʃəp] n.

调味番茄酱

例如 Some people like to eat french fries with ketchup. 一些人喜欢把炸薯条和番茄酱一起吃。

handcart
['hænd,kɑːt] n.

手推车，也可简称为cart。

例如 Supermarkets provide free handcarts for customers. 超市为客人提供免费的手推车。

Philadelphia
[,filə'delfjə; -fiə] n.

美国费城；卡夫菲力奶油芝士。

地道美语

1 bread and butter。直译为"面包和黄油"，但在西方国家日常生活中这是必不可少的生活用品，所以引申为"必不可少的东西"。相信大家都看过电影《朱莉和茱莉亚》，You are the butter to my bread。便是电影中一句经典台词，意为"你是我面包的黄油"（你是我生活中不可或缺的一部分）。例如：

He has a special life style. Surfing and racing is the bread and butter to his life.

他有着很特殊的生活方式。冲浪和赛车是他生活中必不可少的。

2 Buy one and get one for free。买一送一。我们在超市里经常看到打折促销，那么一定要知道买一送一的地道说法。例如：

A: Why did you buy so much olive oil?

B: Today buy one bottle and get another one for free.

A：你为什么买这么多橄榄油?

B：今天买一瓶送一瓶。

3 come along作为动词词组常出现在美语口语中，意为"一起来，一起做……"。可用于征求对方意见，或者邀请对方。例如：

A: When I go shopping, I like a friend to come along.
B: Yeah, a friend gives good advices.

> A：我去购物的时候，喜欢有个朋友跟我一起去。
> B：是啊，朋友总是给出很好的建议。

---

④ **How can that be? 怎么会这样呢？用于表示惊讶或者不相信。学会这种地道的表达方式，就不用一直回答 "really?" 了。例如：**

A: I put the letter on the kitchen table. How can it be gone? How can it be?
B: Don't panic. We will find it.

> A：我把信放在厨房的桌子上了。怎么会不见了呢？
> 怎么会这样呢？
> B：别着急。我们会找到的。

---

⑤ **in your arm's reach. 伸手就拿得到，也引申为某事 "轻而易举"。例如：**

A: You can get an A this year. I know it's in your arm's reach.
B: Don't be so sure. It depends on the questions I get.

> A：你今年能得到A，我知道这对你轻而易举。
> B：别这么肯定。这取决于我拿到什么题目。

6 Supermarkets are springing up like mushrooms. 超市像雨后春笋般涌现出来。注意句中"雨后春笋"的表达。例如：

A: After the new policy is announced, theme parks are springing up like mushrooms.

B: I also noticed, but I don't think every one will be a success.

A：自从新政策出台后，主题公园像雨后春笋般涌现出来。

B：我也注意到了，但是我认为不是每个主题公园都可以成功。

表达方式百宝箱

本课我们学习了和朋友提议一起去购物和在超市购物时的用语，现在就让我们一起来回顾和总结一下吧！

Come along. 一起来，一起做……

How can that be? 怎么会这样呢？

Spring up like mushrooms. 像雨后春笋般涌现。

You are the butter to my bread. 你是我生活中不可缺少的一部分。

小丫 带你走遍美国

奶酪的秘密

制作奶酪的主要原料是牛奶，而牛奶是一种公认的营养佳品。制作1Kg的奶酪大约需要10Kg的牛奶，因此，奶酪又被称为"奶黄金"。奶酪中含有钙、磷、镁、钠等人体必需的矿物质。由于奶酪加工工艺的需要，会添加钙离子，使钙的含量增加，易被人体吸收。下面我们就来了解一下奶酪的种类：

新鲜奶酪：不经过成熟加工处理，直接将牛乳凝固后，去除部分水分而成。质感柔软湿润，散发出清新的奶香与淡淡的酸味，十分爽口。

白霉奶酪：表皮覆盖着白色的真菌绒毛，食用时可以保持表皮的霉菌，也可以根据口味去除。质地十分柔软，奶香浓郁。

蓝纹奶酪：在青霉素的作用下形成大理石花纹般的蓝绿色纹路，味道比起白霉奶酪来显得辛香浓烈，很刺激。

水洗软质奶酪：成熟期需要以盐水或当地特产酒频繁擦洗，表皮呈橙红色，内部柔软，口感醇厚，香气浓郁。

硬质未熟奶酪：制造过程中强力加压并去除部分水分。口感温和爽口。

硬质成熟奶酪：制作时需要挤压和煮，质地坚硬，香气甘美，耐人寻味。可以长时间运送与保存。

山羊奶酪：最经典的山羊奶酪的制法与新鲜奶酪制法相同，可新鲜食用，或去水后食用。体积小巧，形状多样，味道略酸。

当然，上面介绍的只是主要的几种奶酪，有些奶酪根据制作人的精心设计添加坚果或罗勒叶等香料调节口味。有些奶酪是硬质的，一些是软质可涂抹的。奶酪是西方饮食中必不可少的重要部分，小丫想要了解真正的美国文化，吃奶酪是个很好的开始哦。

第11课

吃西餐: 点牛排

情景介绍: 大家都知道, 西餐和中餐不论是在烹饪方法还是在餐桌礼仪方面都截然不同。那么如何吃西餐就成了大家的疑问, 小丫今天要和汤姆去餐厅吃饭, 让我们来看看他们是怎么解决这个问题的吧!

会话1

Tom: Good evening, sir. May I have a table for two, please?

Waiter: Good evening, sir. With reservation or not?

Tom: No reservation.

Waiter: Wait a minute. I'll check. A table for two by the window, this way please.

Tom and Ya: Thank you.

Waiter: Good evening. Here are the menus, and we also have suggestion of the day by the chef. Take your time.

Ya: I don't really understand the menu. Can you explain to me?

Tom: No problem. On the first page, you have the starters, like a salad or a soup. Then you have the main course, including steak or fish, and you always have mashed potato on the side. On the last page, you can see dessert. We like to end a meal with something sweet, but it's not necessary.

Ya: I see. What's this one?

Tom: That's the wine list. You can order aperitif from the list.

Ya: I see. I think I know what I want now.

Waiter: May I have your order, please?

Ya: Yes, I would like a soup of the day and a T-bone steak.

Waiter: How do you want your steak, miss?

Ya: I'd like it medium.

Waiter: And for you, sir?

Tom: Do you have any recommendation for the main course?

Waiter: Certainly. Our suggestion today is the baked codfish filet.

Tom: It's a good idea. I'll take the codfish filet. And to start, I'd like a tuna salad.

Waiter: What would you like to drink?

Ya: For me, a fresh orange juice.

Tom: For me , a glass of white wine, please.

Waiter: How do you want your potato, mashed, boiled or baked?

Ya: Mashed potato for me, please.

Tom: Me, too.

(After the main course)

Waiter: Would you like a dessert?

Ya: A passionfruit sorbet for me, please.

Tom: For me, a chocolate mousse and an espresso.

(After dinner)

Tom: May I have the bill, please?

Waiter: Certainly. Here you are, sir.

Ya: Let's share the bill.

Tom: No, today it's my treat. It's your first western dinner. Next time, you can treat me in the Chinese restaurant.

Ya: Do we leave a tip?

Tom: Yes, normally the tip is 10% of the bill.

汤姆：晚上好，先生。有两个人的位子吗？

服务员：晚上好，先生。是否有预订？

汤姆：没有预订。

服务员：请稍等，我看一下。一张靠窗双人桌，这边请。

汤姆和小丫：谢谢。

服务员：晚上好。这里是菜单，我们也有今天的"主厨推荐"。请你们慢慢选择。

小丫：我不太明白菜单写的是什么。你能给我讲解一下吗？

汤姆：没问题。在第一页上，你看见的是开胃菜，像沙拉或者汤。然后是主菜，包括牛排或者鱼，当然一般主菜都是跟土豆泥一起食用的。在最后一页上，有甜点。我们喜欢用甜点来结束一餐，但甜点不是必需的。

小丫：我知道了。这个是什么？

汤姆：这是酒水单。你可以在酒水单上选择开胃酒。

小丫：我明白了。我想我现在知道点什么了。

服务员：请问可以点餐了吗？

小丫：是的，我想要一份今日例汤和一份T骨牛排。

服务员：您想要牛排几分熟呢，小姐？

小丫：我要半分熟吧。

服务员：您呢，先生？

汤姆：对于主菜你有什么推荐吗？

服务员：当然了，我们今天主推煎鳕鱼。

汤姆：听起来不错。我来一份煎鳕鱼。前菜呢，我要一份金枪鱼沙拉。

服务员：你们要喝点什么呢？

小丫：我要一杯鲜橙汁。

汤姆：请给我来一杯白葡萄酒。

服务员：你们想要哪种土豆泥，煮土豆还是煎土豆？

小丫：请给我来一份土豆泥。

汤姆：我也一样。

（吃过主菜后）

服务员：你们想要饭后甜点吗？

小丫：请给我来一杯西番莲冰沙。

汤姆：我要一个巧克力慕斯和一杯浓缩咖啡。

（吃过晚饭后）

汤姆：麻烦您，结下账。

服务员：给您账单，先生。

小丫：我们平摊吧。

汤姆：不行，今天是我请客。这是你第一次吃西餐。下次我们去中餐馆你请我。

小丫：我们给小费吗？

汤姆：是的，一般是账单的10%。

必备词汇

aperitif
[ə,periti:f] n.

餐前酒，开胃酒

在西方国家，人们正式吃饭之前一般都会喝一小杯开胃酒，酒精含量比较低，而且味道偏甜。

例如 I'd like an aperitif before dinner. 我喜欢在餐前来杯开胃酒。

bake
[beik] v.

烤，烘焙，相当于中式烹调中的煎。

bill
[bil] n.

账单，票据

chef
[ʃef] n.

主厨，厨师长
在西方国家喜欢称主厨，而在我国习惯称为厨师长。

codfish
[ˈkɔdˌfiʃ] n.

鳕鱼

dessert
[diˈzəːt] n.

饭后甜点，甜点
西方饮食中习惯以甜点结束一餐，甜点的种类有很多，有蛋糕、慕斯、冰激凌和沙冰等形式。

reservation
[ˌrezəˈveiʃən] n.

预订，预订的房间或位置，保留
有时去宾馆或餐厅之前需要预订，以保证可以选择自己喜欢的房间或位置。 **例如** This restaurant only accepts reservation a week in advance. 这家餐厅只接受提前一周的预订。

espresso
[eˈspresəu] n.

浓缩咖啡
饭后一杯咖啡也是西方人的饮食习惯之一。

filet
[fiˈlei] n.

肉片，鱼片，猪、牛等的里脊

汉语中常翻译为菲力，其实是音译的。西餐中出现的鱼肉很少有骨头，和中国烹调截然不同。

main course
[kɔːs] n.

主菜，大菜

主要以肉类为主，有牛排、羊排或者鱼类，一般配有蔬菜和土豆泥。

starter
[ˈstɑːtə] n.

前菜，开胃菜，第一道菜

西餐中一般分为前菜、主菜和甜点三部分。前菜以凉菜居多，但也有热汤，分量比较小。

steak
[steik] n.

牛排，肉排，鱼排

T-bone steak是顶骨牛排，T型肋骨的两侧，一侧为莎朗牛排，另一侧为菲力牛排。

tip
[tip] n.

小费

在西方国家，餐厅吃饭后一般会给服务员小费，金额在账单金额的10%至15%之间。

medium [ˈmiːdiəm,
-djəm] adj.

五分熟的

牛排的生熟程度，分为rare、medium和well done三种基本程度，意为三分熟、五分熟和全熟。

passionfruit n.

西番莲，也称为热情果。
是一种热带水果，在西餐烹饪中常常出现，用来当作饭后甜点。

sorbet ['sɔːbət, -bei, sɔː'bei] n.

果汁冰水
这是西餐中较受欢迎的甜点形式之一。

mashed potato [mæʃt] n.

土豆泥

地道美语

1. **by the window** 靠窗。方位的指示语，不一定只是用在餐厅内，也可以用在家里、学校里等其他任何地方。类似的，**by the entrance** 意为"靠门边"。其他方位还有 **in the middle**（在中间），**in the corner**（在角落），**next to the bar**（在吧台旁边）。例如：

A: Do you have a TV in your apartment?
B: Sure. It stands by the window.

    A：你的公寓里有电视吗？
    B：当然啦，就在窗边。

2. **Do you have any recommendation for the main course?** 对于主菜你有什么主推的吗？在西餐厅，一般由当日的主厨

推荐，也就是当日比较有特色的菜品，对于菜单内容和每日推荐，服务员都要烂熟于心，在顾客不知如何选择时给出恰当的建议。例如：

Customer: What are the desserts for today?

Waiter: Well, the suggestion of the day is chocolate cake with whipped cream. Of course, our strawberry mousse has always been a hit.

Customer: I'll take the strawberry mousse then.

客人：今天的甜点都有什么呢？

服务员：今天的甜点推荐是巧克力蛋糕配鲜奶油。当然了，我们的草莓慕斯一直都很受欢迎。

客人：那我来一份草莓慕斯。

注意此例中出现了 whipped cream 和 mousse，这是西餐甜品中经常使用的方式，分别意为"鲜奶油"和"慕斯"。慕斯是一种奶冻式的甜点，质地柔软，入口即化，在西方国家很受欢迎。另外，此例中出现的 be a hit，意为"受欢迎，流行的人或事物"。例如：Nowadays, Justin Bieber is a hit. 当下，贾斯丁·比伯大受欢迎。

③ It's my treat. 我请客，我埋单。西方国家也不是像我们想的那样一直 AA 制，有时在亲戚朋友之间也互相请客。例如：

A: It's my treat today, to celebrate mom's birthday.

B: All right. Thank you for treating us.

A：我请客，庆祝妈妈的生日。

B：好吧，谢谢你请我们。

④ May I have a table for two, please? 有两个人的位子吗？在西方国家，去餐厅吃饭时会先问是否有位置。服务员会问"是否有预订" With reservation or without? 例如：

Customer: May I have a table for four, please?

Waiter: Do you have a reservation, Madam?

Customer: Yeah, under the name Scavo.

Waiter: Sure. This way please, Mrs, Scavo.

客人：有四个人的位子吗？

服务员：女士，您有预订吗？

客人：是的，是斯卡沃的名字预订的。

服务员：好的。请这边走，斯卡沃太太。

5 May I have the bill, please? **请给我结一下账，好吗？吃完饭准备离开时的结账用语，也可以直接说The bill, please。例如：**

Customer: The bill, please.

Waiter: Right away, sir.

客人：结一下账，谢谢。

服务员：马上就来，先生。

表达方式百宝箱

在本课中我们学习了很多有关西餐以及在餐厅吃饭的用语，现在就让我们一起来总结一下吧！

By the window. 靠窗。

It's my treat. 我请客。

May I have a table for two, please? 可以给我一张两个人的桌子吗？

May I have the bill, please? 请给我结一下账好吗？

Starter, main course and dessert. 前菜，主菜和甜点。

小丫 带你走遍 美国

西餐的礼仪

　　就座时，身体要端正，手肘不要放在桌面上，不可跷足，与餐桌的距离以便于使用餐具为佳。餐台上已摆好的餐具不要随意摆弄，一般如果是三道菜的西餐，会由外向内摆好每道菜的刀叉，如果有汤会摆勺子。使用刀叉进餐时，从外侧往内侧取用刀叉，要左手持叉，右手持刀；进餐中放下刀叉时应摆成"八"字型，分别放在餐盘边上。刀刃朝向自身，表示还要继续吃。每吃完一道菜，将刀叉并拢放在盘中，表示不再吃了。如果是谈话，可以拿着刀叉，无须放下。不用刀时，可用右手持叉，但若需要做手势时，就应放下刀叉，千万不可手执刀叉在空中挥舞摇晃，也不要一手拿刀或叉，而另一只手拿餐巾擦嘴，也不可一手拿酒杯，另一只手拿叉取菜。

　　面包一般掰成小块送入口中，抹黄油和果酱时也要先将面包掰成小块再抹，不要拿着整块面包去咬。喝咖啡时如愿意添加牛奶或糖，添加后要用小勺搅拌均匀，将小勺放在咖啡的碟子上，喝时应右手拿杯把，左手端碟子，直接用嘴喝，千万不要用小勺一勺一勺地舀着喝，也不要将小勺留在杯子里。吃水果时，不要拿着水果整个去咬，应先用水果刀切成四瓣再用刀去掉皮、核、用叉子叉着吃。吃鱼、肉等带刺或骨的菜肴时，不要直接外吐，可用餐巾捂嘴轻轻吐在叉上放入盘内。如盘内剩余少量菜肴时，不要用叉子刮盘底，更不要用手指相助食用，应以小块面包或叉子相助食用。吃面条时要用叉子先将面条卷起，然后送入口中。

　　看来，西餐的讲究还真不少呢，希望我们的小丫能够尽快地融入美国文化。

第12课

去医院：发烧真难受

情景介绍： 出国留学去医院是最让人头疼的事情之一，医药费高是一个问题，语言也是一大问题，很多医学术语是我们学习中不曾出现过的。小丫最近发烧，还是去医院检查一下吧，以免延误了病情导致病情加重，我们来看看小丫是如何和医生交流的吧。

会话1

Ya: I don't feel good, so I want to see a doctor.

Nurse: Have you been here before?

Ya: No, this is my first visit.

Nurse: Have you got a registration card?

Ya: No, I don't have one.

Nurse: I will make one for you right now, so it's easier for you for the future visits.

Ya: Thanks.

Nurse: Here is your card, and on the bottom you can see your card number. In every visit, the doctor will put the information in your file, and we can track it with the card number.

Ya: I see.

Nurse: Which department do you want to register with?

Ya: I want to see a surgeon, because I have the fever.

Nurse: Yes, I'll put you in the surgical department. It's on the second floor, on the left side of the elevator.

Ya: Thank you very much!

小丫： 我不舒服，想看医生。

护士： 请问您以前来过本院吗？

小丫： 没来过，这是我第一次来。

护士： 您有挂号卡吗？

小丫： 我没有。

护士： 我现在就给您开一个，以后再来医院比较方便。

小丫： 谢谢。

护士： 这是您的卡，在卡的底部您可以看见卡号。每次来看病，医生都会把信息输入到您的档案里，我们可以用卡号来查询您的信息。

小丫：　我知道了。

护士：　您想挂哪个科室呢？

小丫：　我想挂外科，因为我发烧了。

护士：　好的，我帮你挂外科。在二楼，电梯左侧。

小丫：　非常感谢！

会话2

Doctor: Please have a seat. How can I help you?

Ya: I'm coughing for a few days, and my nose is running, too.

Doctor: I see. Do you have a temperature?

Ya: Yesterday I did, and it was 38 degrees.

Doctor: How much have you been coughing? Have you any sputum?

Ya: I have a bad, dry cough, especially at night. I haven't been sleeping well. Sometimes I vomit after coughing.

Doctor: Do you have a sore throat?

Ya: Yes, I have a lot of pain when eating solid food.

Doctor: I see. Now I'm going to do a brief check.

(After the check)

Doctor: It's most likely a virus infection. I'll give you a prescription. The white tablet is for the fever, but only take it when your temperature is above 38, not more than once in every four hours. The other pill is for the coughing, one teaspoonful

three times a day. However, this coughing pill has some side effects, so stop taking it when your coughing gets better.

Ya: Ok, I will remember them. Thanks, doctor.

Doctor: You are welcome. I hope you will get well soon.

医生：　请坐。有什么可以帮你的吗？

小丫：　我已经咳嗽有几天了，而且一直流鼻涕。

医生：　嗯，我知道了。你发烧吗？

小丫：　是的，昨天发烧38度。

医生：　咳得厉害吗？有痰吗？

小丫：　咳得很厉害，而且是干咳，尤其在晚上的时候，所以我最近的睡眠很不好。有时咳完还会吐。

医生：　嗓子疼吗？

小丫：　是的，吃固体东西的时候嗓子很疼。

医生：　我知道了，现在我来做个简单的检查。

（检查完以后）

医生：　很有可能是病毒感染，我给你开个处方。白色的药片是退烧用的，但是只有在38度以上的时候才服用，而且每次服用要间隔4小时以上。另一种药是止咳的，每日三次，每次一汤匙。但是止咳药有副作用，所以咳嗽一有好转就不要吃了。

小丫： 好的，我会记住的。谢谢你，医生。

医生： 不客气，希望你早日康复。

必备词汇

a sore throat
[sɔ:] [θrəut] n.

嗓子疼

如果按照字面翻译，也许好多读者会说a painful throat，其实这样是不正确的说法。

例如 I think I'm having a cold, because my throat is very sore. 我觉得我感冒了，因为我的嗓子很疼。

surgeon
['sə:dʒən] n.

外科医生

例如 He was afraid of blood when he was young, but he ended up being a surgeon. 他小时候怕血，长大后却成了一名外科医生。

cough
[kɔ:f] v.

咳嗽；n. 咳嗽，咳嗽声

例如 He coughs every day because of smoking too much. 他每天咳嗽，因为抽太多烟了。

vomit
['vɔmit] v.

呕吐，吐出

例如 Vomitting is one of the symptoms of food poisoning. 呕吐是食物中毒的症状之一。注意vomit的-ing形式是vomitting，symptom意为"症状"，食物中毒译为"food poisoning"。

surgical department ['di'pɑ:tmənt] n.

外科

file ['fail] n.

文件，档案

例如 We can see your information in the file. 我们可以在档案里看到你的信息。

prescription [pri'skripʃən] n.

处方，药方

例如 Some medicines are only available with the prescription from the doctor. 有些药只能凭医生的处方才能购买。

side effect n.

副作用

例如 There's no medicine without side effects. 毫无副作用的药几乎没有！

tablet ['tæblit] n.

药片，片剂

例如 These tablets are to keep the fever down. 这些药片是退烧用的。

track [træk] v.

追踪，跟踪

The police tracked the record of what has done and where he has been, so they finally caught him. 对于他的一举一动以及动向，警方了如指掌，最终将他绳之以法。

virus infection ['vairəs] [in'fekʃən] n.

病毒感染

例如 Flu is a kind of virus infection. 流感是一种病毒感染。

teaspoonful ['ti:,spu:nful] n.

一茶匙的量

相对应的是tablespoonful n. 一满勺，一大汤匙的量。用于衡量液体的量词。

例如 People shouldn't eat more than one teaspoonful of sugar every day. 人每天食用的糖不应该超过一茶匙的量。

elevator ['eliveitə] n.

电梯，升降机

英式英语中称为lift。我们在商场中使用的自动扶梯是escalator，二者不要混淆。例如 Many department stores have both elevators and escalators. 很多百货公司既有电梯又有自动扶梯。

地道美语

① **Do you have a temperature? 发烧吗？ 这是医生常用的问法，而并不是问Do you have a fever? 例如：**

Doctor: Do you have a temperature?

Patient: I don't think so, but I have been sweating very much.

医生：你发烧吗？

病人：我觉得不发烧，但是我出很多汗。

2 Have you got a registration card? 你有挂号卡吗？在美国医院一般要持在此医院注册的挂号卡就医，卡上记录有个人信息和就医信息。registration在这里意为"挂号"。例如：

Nurse: Could you tell me the number of your registration card, miss?

Patient: Sorry, but I don't have a card yet. It's my first visit to this hospital.

护士：小姐，能告诉我你的挂号卡的卡号吗？

病人：对不起，我还没有挂号卡。这是我第一次来你们医院。

3 My nose is running. 我一直流鼻涕。running nose意为"流鼻涕"，好像鼻子在跑，既形象又生动。例如：

A: Every time I eat spicy food, I will have a running nose.

B: It's the same as me, and I also have a sore throat.

A：每次我吃辣的食物都会流鼻涕。

B：我也是这样，而且我还会嗓子疼。

4 This is my first visit. 这是我第一次来。美语中表达简洁，比如这句地道的美语不会说"It's the first time I came here."而且句中的visit是不需要翻译出来的。例如：

A: Have you seen the fantastic paintings on the second floor?

B: Not yet, it's my first visit.

A：你看到二楼墙上的画了吗？真是太美了！

B：还没呢，这是我第一次来。

5 Which department do you want to register with? 你想挂哪个科? 英语中一个科室称为department n. 部门，系，科。例如：

A: When a child is sick, he or she should be taken to paediatrician.

B: That's right. They are specialized in children's health.

A：如果小孩生病了，他（她）应该去看儿科医生。

B：是的，他们是儿童健康的专家。

表达方式百宝箱

本课中我们学习了在医院挂号的用语，以及与医生交谈时可能出现的问题，里面不乏专业医疗术语，所以现在就让我们一起来总结一下吧！

Do you have a sore throat? 嗓子疼吗?

Do you have a temperature? 发烧吗?

Have you got a registration card? 你有挂号卡吗?

How much have you been coughing? 咳得厉害吗?

I have a bad, dry cough, especially at night. 我咳得很厉害，而且是干咳，夜里尤其严重。

I hope you will get well soon. 我希望你早日康复。

My nose is running. 我一直流鼻涕。

This is my first visit. 这是我第一次来。

小丫 带你走遍 美国

在美国就医

美国的医院分为公立医院和私立医院两种。

公立医院保证居民的基本医疗，属于平民阶层，病人看完病或做完检查后可以拒绝支付账单，当然指的是由政府花钱救治的重症患者或无任何保险的非法移民等。美国的做法是先看病和做必要的检查，服务后将账单给病人，但付钱与否由患者决定。医院的所有费用，特别是最为昂贵的人力支出由政府财政预算拨款，患者付钱与否不影响医务人员的收入。每年的州议会会委托会计师事务所对郡立医院的财政支出和每个学科的医疗费用进行审计，并向州议会计交财务报告，以决定新财政年度的医院预算。

私立医院的资金来源主要有三种：1. 患者支付的医疗费用。绝大部分是保险公司支付的款项。2. 研究经费和衍生收益。美国的一流医院承担着众多的科研开发、试制和临床试验工作。往往几家医院的多中心研究结果左右着FDA的政策导向和诸多公司的财务状况，所以各大药厂在临床试验和前期研发的投入十分惊人。另外，投入的很大一部分是由大型医院的实验室承担的。在药品和各种医疗设备开发成功并投入市场后，其价值回报也是私立医院重要的收入来源之一。3. 各种捐助和投资，全美不计其数的私人基金会和慈善机构每年都向医院系统捐助数以百亿计的资金，用于医学研究和帮助那些需要帮助的患者。

中美的医院体系和医疗制度都有很大差别。要想在美国长期生活，了解就医程序是十分必要的，希望我们的小丫早日康复。

第13课

咖啡的秘密

情景介绍: 大家都知道西方国家崇尚喝咖啡,那么真正的咖啡是不是和我们平常喝到的雀巢咖啡一样呢?今天,小丫和汤姆就要在咖啡厅见面,让我们来看看美国人到底是怎么喝咖啡的吧!

会话1

Tom: Are you up for a cup of coffee in a cozy Café?

Ya: Absolutely! I want to see how coffee and Café are in America.

Tom: There's one close to my apartment. Jerry and I often go there.

Waiter: Welcome. Please have a seat. Here is the menu.

Tom and Ya: Thank you.

Waiter: What drinks can I get for you?

Tom: I'd like a coffee Mocha.

Ya: I will take a coffee Latte.

Waiter: Here you are. Enjoy.

Ya: What's the difference between different coffees?

Tom: Well, that's a long story. Firstly, you have regular coffee, such as Colombian coffee, Blue Mountain coffee. Then it comes to coffees like Irish coffee, Vienna coffee and Ice coffee, which have syrup, whipped cream or some alcohol to supplement the taste. Thirdly, you have Italian coffee, including Espresso, Macchiatto, Latte, Cappuccino, Mocha, Caramel Macchiatto and others. Of course there's also coffee Americano, which means American coffee.

Ya: Wow! There are so many kinds of coffee. I knew coffee from Starbucks in China, and the instant Neste coffee.

Tom: China is more a country of tea. We are used to the taste of coffee, and for some people a morning coffee is necessary.

Ya: What's the difference between all Italian coffees?

Tom: The difference mostly lies in the amount of milk. Espresso is without milk at all, but espresso is the basis of all coffees. Then it comes to Macchiatto, which has some milk foam on top. Next, it comes to Latte, which is espresso with milk and milk foam. After Macchiatto, you have Cappuccino, which is also espresso with milk and milk foam, but compared to Latte its milk is less and milk foam is more. Then you have Mocha, which is espresso with chocolate syrup, milk and whipped cream. Sounds yummy, doesn't it? Finally you have Caramel Macchiatto, which is espresso with milk foam, syrup and caramel above.

Ya: Sounds a bit complicated to me.

Tom: It's normal. But after you get used to the coffee taste, I'm sure you will know all the differences.

Ya: I hope so.

汤姆: 有没有兴趣去一家舒适的咖啡厅喝杯咖啡?

小丫: 当然啦!我想看看真正的美国咖啡和咖啡厅是什么样子。

汤姆: 在我的公寓旁边有一家,杰瑞和我经常光顾。

服务员: 欢迎光临。请坐。这是菜单。

汤姆和小丫: 谢谢。

服务员: 你们要喝点什么呢?

汤姆: 我要一个摩卡咖啡。

小丫: 我要一个拿铁咖啡。

服务员: 你们的咖啡。请慢用。

小丫： 不同咖啡之间的区别是什么呢？

汤姆： 哎呀，这个说起来话就长了。首先，我们有一般咖啡，比如哥伦比亚咖啡、蓝山咖啡。然后是像爱尔兰咖啡、维也纳咖啡和冰咖啡这样的花式咖啡，里面有糖浆、鲜奶油或者少量酒来增补味道。再次，有意大利咖啡，包括浓缩咖啡、玛奇朵、拿铁、卡布奇诺、摩卡、焦糖玛奇朵和一些其他的。当然也有美式咖啡。

小丫： 哇！咖啡居然有这么多种类。我以前只是从中国的星巴克和雀巢咖啡知道咖啡的。

汤姆： 中国是一个饮茶的国家。我们习惯了咖啡的味道，并且对一些人来说每天早晨一杯咖啡是必要的。

小丫： 那么不同的意大利咖啡之间有什么区别呢？

汤姆： 主要区别是放牛奶量的不同。浓缩咖啡里面是没有加任何牛奶的，当然它也是所有咖啡的基础。然后是玛奇朵，是浓缩咖啡上加奶泡。接下来是拿铁，它是浓缩咖啡上加牛奶，牛奶上再加奶泡。然后是卡布奇诺，它也是浓缩咖啡加牛奶跟奶泡，但跟拿铁的区别是牛奶比较少，奶泡比较多。再下面是摩卡，它是浓缩咖啡上加巧克力糖浆，上面加牛奶和鲜奶油。听起来很美味，不是吗？最后是焦糖玛奇朵，是浓缩咖啡加奶泡，糖浆，最上面再加焦糖。

小丫： 听起来有点复杂。

汤姆： 这很正常。但是当你习惯咖啡的味道以后，我相信你就知道这里面的区别了。

小丫： 希望如此。

必备词汇

Cappuccino
[ˌkæpuˈtʃiːnəu] n.

卡布奇诺咖啡

20世纪初，意大利人阿奇加夏发明蒸汽压力咖啡机的同时，也发明了卡布奇诺咖啡。卡布奇诺是在浓缩咖啡上，倒入以蒸汽发泡的牛奶。此时咖啡的颜色，就像卡布奇诺教会的修士在深褐色的外衣上覆上一条头巾一样，咖啡因此而得名。

cozy
[ˈkəuzi] adj.

舒适的，舒服的，安逸的

这是美式口语中常用的词，比起comfortable是不是简洁也地道得多呢。**例如** Guests can relax in the cozy bar in this hotel. 这家酒店的客人可以在温暖舒适的酒吧休息。

instant
[ˈinstənt] adj.

立即的，紧急的

我们日常生活中的方便面称为"instant noodles"，速溶咖啡称为"instant coffee"。

yummy
[ˈjʌmi] adj.

好吃的，美味的

类似说法还有tasty和nice，美国人在口语中基本不说delicious，而这个词在中国已经被滥用了。**例如** The chicken in my salad is tender and yummy. 我的沙拉里面的鸡肉很嫩，而且很好吃。

Latte
['lɑːtei] n.

拿铁咖啡

拿铁咖啡是意大利浓缩咖啡与牛奶的经典混合。"拿铁"是意大利文"Latte"的译音，拿铁咖啡(Coffee Latte)是花式咖啡的一种，是咖啡与牛奶混合的极至之作，意式拿铁咖啡纯为牛奶加咖啡，美式拿铁则将牛奶替换成奶泡。

Macchiatto n.

玛奇朵咖啡

Macchiatto在意大利语中是一点点的意思，在一小杯Espresso中直接加入一两勺奶泡，一杯玛奇朵就做成了。Caramel Macchiatto n. 焦糖玛奇朵咖啡。

Mocha
['mɔkə; 'məukə] n.

摩卡咖啡

摩卡是一种最古老的咖啡，其历史要追溯到咖啡的起源，得名于有名的摩卡港。15世纪，只要是集中到摩卡港再向外输出的非洲咖啡，都被统称为摩卡咖啡。后来新兴的港口虽然代替了摩卡港的地位，但是摩卡港时期摩卡咖啡的产地依然保留了下来，这些产地所产的咖啡豆，仍被称为摩卡咖啡豆。

syrup
['sirəp, 'səː-] n.

糖浆；含药糖浆

例如 Some people like to eat bread with syrup. 一些人喜欢在面包上涂糖浆吃。This syrup is good for your cough. 这种糖浆对治疗你的咳嗽很有效。

supplement
['sʌplimənt,
'sʌpləmənt] v.

增补，补充

例如 She got a part-time job to supplement the family income. 她找了一份兼职工作来贴补家用。

地道美语

① **It's my cup of tea.** 是我的口味，是我喜欢的。否定说法为 **It's not my cup of tea.** 这种说法就是我们日常生活中说的"这是/不是我的风格"。例如：

A: I don't want to take this dress. It's not my cup of tea.

B: It's all up to you.

　　A： 我不想买这条裙子，不是我的风格。

　　B： 你自己决定啊。

② **That's a long story.** 说来话长。类似的说法有 **Long story short.** 长话短说。在说一件比较复杂的事情时，可以用此表达方式表示简化说话内容。

Daughter: How did you and mom meet?

Dad: Well, that's a long but very romantic story.

Daughter: You can make the long story short. I'm curious.

　　女儿： 你和妈妈是怎么认识的？

　　爸爸： 这可说来话长，不过很浪漫。

　　女儿： 你可以长话短说嘛，我很好奇。

③ The difference mostly lies in the amount of milk. 区别主要在于所放牛奶的量。注意句中lie的用法，意为"位于，在于，展现"。例如：

Happiness doesn't lie in the significance of possession.
快乐的意义并不在于占有。

④ Yummy. 好吃，美味的。例如：

A: My husband got a promotion, so I'm going to make roasted spring chicken this evening, with fries and salad on the side, and we will also open a bottle of good wine.

B: Mmm, yummy. Congratulations!

A：我丈夫升职了，今天晚上我要做一个烤春鸡，配上薯条和沙拉，我们再开一瓶好酒，庆祝一下。

B：嗯，好吃。祝贺你们哦！

表达方式百宝箱

　　本课中我们学习了有关咖啡的种类，各种咖啡的叫法以及不同咖啡之间的区别，大家要注意复习哦。

It's (not) my cup of tea. （不）是我喜欢的，（不）是我的口味。

Long story short. 长话短说。

That's a long story. 说来话长。

Yummy. 好吃，美味的。

小丫 带你走遍 美国

咖啡的秘密

咖啡(Coffee)一词源自埃塞俄比亚的一个名叫卡法(Kaffa)的小镇，在希腊语中"Kaweh"的意思是"力量与热情"。茶叶与咖啡、可可并称为世界三大饮料。

咖啡出现的最早且最确切的时间是公元前8世纪，但是早在荷马的作品和许多古老的阿拉伯传奇里，就已记述了一种神奇的、色黑、味苦涩、且具有强烈刺激力量的饮料。还有一个源自15世纪的奇特故事，传说一个也门牧羊人看见一群山羊从一丛灌木上吃色泽微红的浆果，很快这些山羊变得焦躁不安、兴奋不已，这个牧羊人把这件事报告给了一位修道士。这位修道士将一些浆果煮熟，然后提炼出一种味苦劲足的、能驱赶困倦和睡意的饮料。

到16世纪时，早期的商人已在欧洲贩卖咖啡，由此将咖啡作为一种新型饮料引入西方的风俗和生活当中。但是随着市场需求的日益增长、进出口港口强加的高额关税，以及人们对咖啡树种植领域知识的增强，经销商和科学家开始尝试把咖啡移植到其他国家。1727年巴西北部开始了咖啡种植，然而糟糕的气候条件使得这种作物种植逐渐转移到了其他区域，最初是里约热内卢，最后到了圣保罗和米纳斯州，在这里咖啡找到了它最理想的生长环境。咖啡种植在这里发展壮大，直到成为巴西最重要的经济来源之一。虽然咖啡诞生于非洲，但是种植和家庭消费却相对来说是近代才引进的。实际上，正是欧洲人让咖啡重返故地，将其引进他们的殖民地，在那里，由于有利的土地和气候条件，咖啡才得以兴旺繁荣。

如果要把有关咖啡的故事都讲完，那真的是一个long story。小丫今天在咖啡厅，不仅体验了美国的下午茶文化，也了解到了有关咖啡的知识，真是收获不小呢。

第14课

买衣服: 选对尺码试试看

情景介绍: 许多留学生在出国之前都买好衣服, 因为国内的价格比较低廉。其实在美国, 大众消费的物价也很低, 与其拖着重重的行李箱远渡重洋, 还不如在美国本地买到称心如意的东西呢。今天小丫要去商场购物, 我们一起来看一看吧!

会话1

Ya: This place is great. I'm surprised they have so many things.

Jessica: Yes, but it takes a while to find the things you want. It's not organized as carefully as a regular store.

Ya: I never shopped in an outlet before. Why is it called an "outlet"?

Jessica: Sometimes a clothes company makes too many of one item. They can't sell it all in the regular store. So they send the overstock to an outlet and sell them with a lower price. It's a store that "let out" products that the company can't sell in regular stores.

Ya: Do they also have faulty products here?

Jessica: Yes. A "faulty product" may be a shirt that has some problem. Or a pair of pants that is ripped a little. Most of the time, the fault is very small. So it's a good deal to buy it. Sometimes, if you have a needle and thread, you can fix it yourself.

Ya: I think it's a really good deal. Some of these shirts have only one tiny mistake on them.

Jessica: I know. So it's a good idea to shop in an outlet sometimes. It saves a lot of money for you.

Ya: I like these jeans!

Jessica: What's your size? Let's try it on.

Ya: I don't know the American size, but my size in China is 165.

Jessica: Let's see. In America, we have 2, 4-6, 8-10, 12-14, 16-18. If you are 165, I think it should be 4 or Medium. Let's try.

Ya: You are right. This is the right size for me. I'll take these jeans.

Cashier: Cash or credit card, Miss?

Ya: Credit card, please.

Jessica: Wow! How many pairs did you buy?

Ya: Three. I took different colors. It's really a good deal.

Jessica: You really know how to use an outlet store!

Ya: I ought to make the most of it while I'm here, don't you think?

Jessica: Sure. You are smart.

小丫：　这个地方太棒了！看到这儿有这么多东西我很惊讶。

杰西卡：　是的，但是要找到你想买的东西可能要花上一段时间。它不像一般商场那样井井有条。

小丫：　我从没在"大卖场"购物过。为什么叫大卖场呢？

杰西卡：　有时服装公司一种款式生产太多，不能把所有的产品都在一般商店卖完。所以他们把存货拿到大卖场来卖，价格会稍低一点。大卖场就是商家把没卖出去的产品清出去的地方。

小丫：　这儿也有瑕疵产品吗？

杰西卡：　是的，瑕疵产品可能是一件有点小毛病的衬衫，或者一条有破损的裤子。大多数时候都是很小的瑕疵，所以是很值得购买的。有时如果你有针线，自己就可以解决。

小丫：　我觉得是很值得购买的，这些衬衫上只有很小的瑕疵。

杰西卡：　我知道。所以有时在大卖场购物是很好的主意，可以省下不少钱。

小丫： 我喜欢这些牛仔裤。

杰西卡： 穿多大码？我们来试试看。

小丫： 我不知道美国的尺码，但是我在中国时尺码是165。

杰西卡： 让我想想。在美国我们有2号、4-6号、8-10号、12-14号、16-18号。如果你是165的话，我觉得应该是4号或者中号。我们来试试。

小丫： 你说对了，这正是我的尺码。我要买这些牛仔裤。

收银员： 现金还是刷卡，小姐？

小丫： 刷卡，谢谢。

杰西卡： 哇！你买了多少条同款的牛仔裤啊？

小丫： 三条，我买了不同颜色。很值得的。

杰西卡： 你可真会逛大卖场。

小丫： 我应该趁着来这儿好好利用机会，不是吗？

杰西卡： 当然对啦，你真聪明。

必备词汇

faulty ['fɔːlti] adj.

有错误的，有缺点的

例如 In a second-hand shop, you can often find faulty goods, but most of them are used. 在二手商店，你总能找到瑕疵商品，而且他们大多数都是被使用过的。

pants [pænts] n.

裤子，裤装

是美国口语中的日常用语，比起trousers要轻松地道得多。

例如 Young girls like to wear hot pants now. 现在的年轻女孩喜欢穿热裤。

cashier
[kæˈʃiə] n.

收银员，收款员，收银台

例如 The supermarket needs more cashiers now. 这家超市现在招聘收银员。

item
[ˈaitəm] n.

商品，物品

例如 Most export companies have a catalogue of all the items they have. 大多数出口公司都有所有商品的目录。

jeans
[dʒiːnz] n.

牛仔裤

这是一个单复数同形的名词，但是没有a jeans，只有a pair of jeans，使用方法与trousers相同。**例如** Levi's is famous for their jeans. 李维斯以牛仔裤出名。

needle and thread
[ˈniːdl] [θred] n.

针线

ought to
[ɔːt]

应该，理应，应当

例如 You ought to do some sports before your weight gets out of control. 你应该在体重失控之前做做运动。

outlet
[ˈaut,let, -lit] n.

大卖场，折扣店

例如 Many tourists in Hong Kong go shopping in the outlets. 来香港的很多游客去折扣店购物。

overstock
[ˌəuvəˈstɔk,
ˌəuvəstɔk] n.

过多的存货，过多的库存

例如 They have overstock of Christmas cards. 他们的圣诞节贺卡还有很多的库存。

地道美语

1 It's a good deal. **值得购买。意为"很便宜，很划算"。类似说法还有** It's a good buy. **和** It's a good bargain. **例如：**

A: Jane is very good at bargaining. Every time I go shopping with her, I can get good deals.

B: I know. I love going shopping with her!

A：简真擅长讲价。我每次跟她去购物，总是能买到物美价廉的东西。

B：我知道，我特别爱跟她一起购物！

2 Let's try it on. **让我们穿上试试看。** try it on **是指买衣服或者鞋子时的试穿。英语中的试衣间称为** fitting room。**例如：**

A: Can you get a pair of 37 for me? I'd like to try them on.

B: Sure, Ma'am. Wait a second.

A：你能帮我找一双37码的吗？我想试试看。

B：没问题，女士。请稍等一下。

3 I ought to make the most of it. 我应该充分利用。注意句中 make the most of something 意为"尽量利用，充分利用"。例如：

A: You are more beautiful and happier than ever.

B: I just want to make the most of my youth.

A：你现在比任何时候都美丽和快乐。

B：我只是想充分利用青春时光。

4 You always have ants in your pants! 你总是像只热锅上的蚂蚁。表示某人坐立不安的状态。例如：

A: Calm down. It's like you have ants in your pants.

B: I can't. I'm really nervous right now.

A：冷静点，你像只热锅上的蚂蚁。

B：我冷静不了，现在我真的很紧张。

表达方式百宝箱

本课中我们学习了有关购物的表达方式，现在就让我们一起来总结一下吧！

It's a good deal. 很值得购买，很划算。

Let's try it on. 让我们穿上试试看。

I ought to make the most of it. 我应该充分利用。

小丫 带你走遍美国

体验折扣店(Outlet)

折扣店（Outlet）是以销售自有品牌和周转快的商品为主，限定销售品种，并以有限的经营面积、简单的店铺装修和低廉的经营成本，向消费者提供"物有所值"的商品为主要目的的零售方式。

由于经营成本能得到有效控制，在美国的折扣店，消费者们常能得到一两折的购物惊喜。这种间断性的超低价刺激能够持续地保持顾客对折扣店的激情，而经常光顾也会带来计划外的消费，这样消费者既满足了淘到了物美价廉的商品，商家也可以在营业额上有所增加，是何乐不为的双赢局面。尤其在品牌折扣店，即时价格只有原价的50%，消费者还是会觉得是很大的优惠。正是因为有一般商场的原价作为对比，折扣店显得更加适合大众消费，也不存在信用问题。

一般美国的折扣店都开在郊区，这样不仅商场用地的租金比较低廉，也方便开车来的消费者停车和购买大量商品。折扣店的装修和室内设计不会像商场专柜那样别具匠心，而且有时想找到称心如意的商品需要耐心的挑选，就像网上购物需要"淘宝"一样。在美国，许多折扣店都给消费者一个后悔的余地，如果买完后改变了主意还可以退换。

小丫作为留学生，去折扣店购物无疑是个明智的选择，既可以买到质量上乘的商品，又不会担心价格太高，超出学生的负担。

第15课

遭遇警察: 请出示你的证件

情景介绍: 在美国, 在路上开车经常会遇到警察检查身份证件或者严查酒驾。美国人已经见惯不怪了, 但是对于留学生小丫来说, 这些还不曾经历过。今天小丫和汤姆开车出行, 刚好遇到警察的检查, 就让我们来看看到底是怎样的情况吧。

会话1

Ya: There seems to be a bad traffic jam in front.

Tom: Yeah. I wonder what's going on.

Ya: Maybe there's a car accident.

Tom: It's possible. We have many drink and drive problems in the States.

Ya: I see policemen nearby.

Tom: We will see.

Police officer: Please roll down the window.

Tom: What's the matter, sir?

Police officer: We are checking drunk driving on this road right now.

Tom: Ok, I see.

Police officer: You see the cars on the side there? Drivers who have been drinking have to pull their vehicles over there. Have you been drinking?

Tom: No, I haven't, sir.

Police officer: May I have your ID card? And you too, Ma'am.

Tom and Ya: Sure. Here you are, sir.

Police officer: Your driving license as well, sir.

Tom: Oh yes, here it is.

Police officer: Now you need to blow to the breathalyzer.

Tom: It's the first time I do this. How is it done?

Police officer: It's very simple. Just blow very hard, and I'll tell you when to stop.

Tom: All right.

Police officer: You can stop, sir. It says you are sober.

Tom: Sure. I haven't drunk today, and I don't drink when I need to drive. I know how dangerous that is to me and to other people.

Police officer: Indeed. We will have less accidents if all Americans think the same. Here are your ID cards and your driving license. Have a good evening, sir.

Tom: Thank you, sir. Good night.

小丫： 前面堵车很严重。

汤姆： 是啊，我也在想到底发生了什么。

小丫： 可能是一场交通事故。

汤姆： 有可能。在美国我们有很多酒后驾车引起的问题。

小丫： 我看见附近有警察。

汤姆： 我们一会儿就知道了。

警察： 请摇下你的车窗。

汤姆： 怎么了，警官？

警察： 我们正在检查这条路上的酒驾。

汤姆： 哦，我知道了。

警察： 你看见路边上的车了吗？饮酒的司机要把车靠在
那边。你今天有喝酒吗？

汤姆： 不，我今天没喝酒，警官。

警察： 请出示你的身份证，还有你的，女士。

汤姆和小丫： 好的。给你，警官。

警察： 还有你的驾驶执照，先生。

汤姆： 是的，在这儿。

警察： 现在你需要在酒精探测器上吹气。

汤姆： 这是我第一次遇到检查酒驾。我应该怎么做？

警察：很简单。你只需要用力吹气，我会告诉你什么时候停下来的。

汤姆：好的。

警察：你可以停下来了，先生。仪器显示你是清醒的。

汤姆：当然。我今天没喝酒，而且如果开车的话我是不会喝酒的。我知道这样对我自己和对其他人有多危险。

警察：的确如此。如果所有美国人都像你这么想，我们就不会有这么多交通事故了。这是你们的身份证和驾照。晚上愉快，先生。

汤姆：谢谢，警官。祝您晚安。

必备词汇

breathalyzer [ˈbreθəlaizə] n.

体内酒精测定器

例如 Policemen use the breathalyzer to check drunk driving. 警察用体内酒精测定仪来检查酒驾。

pull over [pul] v.

把车开到路边，靠边停车

例如 Can you pull over? I don't feel good. 你能靠边停车吗？我觉得不舒服。

sober [ˈsəubə] adj.

清醒的，未醉的

例如 He drove into the old lady when he was sober. 他撞倒老妇人的时候是清醒的。

roll down [rəul] v.

旋开，摇下

因为老式汽车中的车窗是手摇式的，这种表达方式由此而来。虽然现在的车窗已经不需要手摇了，roll down 还是作为习惯说法保留下来。

例如 He rolled down the window of his car when the girl knocked. 当女孩敲车窗时，他摇下了车窗。

traffic jam [dʒæm] n.

交通堵塞，塞车

例如 There are bad traffic jams in big cities like Beijing and Shanghai, especially during rush hours. 在像北京和上海这样的大城市有很严重的交通堵塞，尤其是上下班高峰时间。

地道美语

1 **What's going on?** 发生什么了？ / 怎么了？这是美国口语中常用的表达方式，表示自己的疑惑不解。例如：

A: What's going on here? How come there are only three people at work today?

B: There's a protest today. You don't know it?

A：怎么了？怎么今天只有三个人来上班？

B：今天有个游行示威。你不知道吗？

2 Drink and drive. 酒后驾车。和drunk driving的意思相同，但是更为口语化。例如：

A: Many people have no idea what problem they will cause by drinking and driving.

B: People always think they'll get lucky this time.

A：许多人不知道酒后驾车能引起什么问题。

B：人们总是觉得这次能走运。

3 What's the matter? 怎么回事？ / 有什么事吗？如果问别人 "What's the matter with you?" 就是有点不礼貌的表达方式了，意为 "你怎么回事？你有什么毛病？" 例如：

A: I think we have a lot to talk about, just like what you need to do with your daughter.

B: What's the matter, mom? Don't get so serious.

A：我觉得我们有很多话需要谈谈，正如你和你女儿之间有许多要谈的一样。

B：怎么了，妈妈？别这么严肃。

4 Sober up! 清醒起来，使……清醒起来，使……严肃起来。类似的表达方式还有Wake up! 并不是真的叫对方醒过来，而是叫对方清醒起来、振作起来。例如：

A: I don't know what has happened. It's so overwhelming lately.

B: I can understand. The best way is to go out and get some fresh air, so you can sober up.

A：我不知道发生了什么。最近发生的有点让我承受不住。

B：我可以理解。最好的办法是去外面走走，呼吸一下新鲜空气，这样你就能清醒起来。

注意例句中的overwhelming，意为"压倒性的，势不可挡的"。用于形容自己难以承受或难以接受的事情。

小丫带你走遍美国

美国的警察

美国的警察主要有联邦、州和市县警察三级。联邦和各州的警察分别行使联邦和州赋予的权力。州以下各种警察的权限由各州决定，除联邦警察外，州警察、城市警察和县警察及私人保安与联邦政府没有垂直的上下关系，直接由地方政府领导。我们主要了解一下大名鼎鼎的联邦调查局和美剧中经常出现的NYPD。

联邦调查局（Federal Bureau of Investigation, FBI）隶属于美国司法部（U.S.Department of Justice），是联邦警察体系中最主要的部门，在美国各地和波多黎各一共分布着56个分局、400个办事处。除此之外，它在外国还设有70个办事处，一共有三万多名雇员。它负责调查200多种违反联邦法律的犯罪行为或严重威胁国家安全的犯罪行为，它的工作权限包括监视、窃听（必须在法院授权下）、调查商业纪录、调查白领的犯罪和参加秘密侦破活动。他们的职权范围包括调查以下几种案件：有组织犯罪，公职腐败，金融犯罪，欺诈政府，行贿受贿，版权侵犯，侵犯公民权利，抢劫银行，敲诈勒索，绑架，劫机，恐怖活动，间谍，州际犯罪，贩卖毒品，以及其他违反联邦法律的犯罪。

NYPD是New York Police Department的简称，即纽约市警察局。它是美国最大，同时也是世界上效率最高、设备最先进的警察局。纽约市警察局成立于1845年，是目前美国最大的警察局，负责纽约市五个区的警力部署及案件调查。它也是美国历史最悠久的警察局。纽约警局的格言是"至死忠诚"（Faithful to Death）。纽约警察局总部设在警察局广场（One Police Plaza），这里拥有打击犯罪的计算机网络，也就是用来协助警探完成调查的巨大的搜索引擎和数据库。根据警察局方面的说法，其任务是要"执法、维和、减少恐慌，并提供一个安全的环境"（enforce the laws, preserve the peace, reduce fear, and provide for a safe environment）。

小丫的美国生活不仅丰富多彩，也充满了意想不到的状况。当然，这些都是小丫成长的必经之路。今天和警察的近距离接触就让小丫更加了解了美国对交通安全的重视与投入。

第16课

热心的纽约人：不担心迷路

情景介绍： 独自来到陌生的国家、陌生的城市求学，有些留学生尽量避免出门，担心自己会迷路。不过这可不是融入当地文化的好办法。即使现在的手机上网和GPS（全球定位系统）很发达，高昂的手机费也是中国留学生所不能承受的。俗话说，嘴长在鼻子下面，问一问自然就知道啦。让我们来看看小丫是如何解决问路难题的吧。

会话1

Ya: Excuse me, Ma'am. Can I ask you something, please?

Ma'am: Yes, of course. Go ahead.

Ya: Where is Sint-Peter Music School?

Ma'am: Sint-Peter Music School? I don't know. I'm also new here.

Ya: Oh, I see. Thanks anyway.

小丫： 打扰一下，女士。我能问您个问题吗？

女士： 当然可以了。你说。

小丫： 圣彼得音乐学校怎么走？

女士： 圣彼得音乐学校？我不知道。我也是新来不久。

小丫： 哦，是这样啊。依然很感谢您。

会话2

Ya: Excuse me. Do you know how to go to Sint-Peter Music School?

Boy: Sint-Peter Music School? It lies in Washington Street, I think.

Ya: Ok. Where is Washington Street then?

Boy: Let me see. Now we are in 16th avenue. You go straight along this street, and then you turn to the first street on the right. At the end of the street you turn left. Then you will be in Washington Street, if everything goes right.

Ya: Thank you very much.

Boy: You are welcome.

小丫： 打扰一下，你知道去圣彼得音乐学校怎么走吗？

男孩： 圣彼得音乐学校？它在华盛顿街上，我觉得。

小丫： 好的，那么华盛顿街怎么走呢？

男孩： 让我想想。我们现在在第十六大街上。你沿着这条路
直走，然后右边第一个路口右转，在那条街的街尾左
转，如果一切顺利的话，那么你就在华盛顿街上了。

小丫： 非常感谢。

男孩： 不客气。

 会话3

Ya: Excuse me, sir. Can you help me?

Man: What can I do for you?

Ya: I'm looking for Central Park Street. Can you tell me how to go there?

Man: That's just in this block. You follow this street till the second crossroad, and then turn to the right. So, straight on, and then right. You see?

Ya: Yeah, it's perfectly clear. Thank you, sir. Have a nice day.

Man: My pleasure. Good luck to you.

小丫： 打扰一下，先生，您可以帮助我吗？

男人： 我可以为你做些什么？

小丫： 我在找中央公园街。您能告诉我怎么去那儿吗？

男人： 中央公园街就在这个街区里。你先沿着这条路直走，到第二个十字路口右转。简单说就是直走，然后右转。明白了吗？

小丫： 明白了，非常清楚。谢谢您，先生。祝您今天愉快。

男人： 很乐意帮助你。祝你好运。

会话4

Ya: Do you know where the post office is?

Girl: It's quite far. You'd better take the subway. There's a stop called City Post, which is the place you are looking for.

Ya: I see. Where's the closest subway station here?

Girl: That's not far. You cross the street, and then go straight for about 5 minutes. There it is.

Ya: That's indeed not far. Thanks.

Girl: No problem.

小丫： 你知道邮局怎么走吗?

女孩： 距离这儿还是很远的。你最好乘地铁去。有一站叫作"城市邮局"，应该正是你要去的地方。

小丫： 我知道了。这里最近的地铁站在哪儿呢?

女孩： 地铁站不远。你过马路，然后直走，大概5分钟就能看见了。

小丫： 确实不太远。谢谢。

女孩： 不客气。

必备词汇

本课中我们主要学习问路的表达方式，以及如何回答，因此生词量很小，主要的词汇请看下面解释与例句。

avenue ['ævənju:] n.

大街，大道

众所周知的"星光大道"称为avenue of stars；美国的广告业中心"麦德逊大道"称为Madison avenue。 **例如** "Fifth Avenue" is a popular jeans brand. "第五大街"是颇受欢迎的牛仔裤品牌。

lie [lai] v.

位于，坐落于

多用于表示城市、建筑物的地理方位。

straight on [streit] adv.

一直往前，往前直走

同义的表达方式还有straight ahead。 **例如** The trucks drove straight on in this heavy weather. 在这种恶劣天气下卡车还是一直往前开。

地道美语

① Go ahead. 前进，进行；说吧，开始吧，开始（做某事）。用于口语中多为"说吧"的意思。例如：

A: There's something I want to talk about with you, but I don't know where to start.

B: Go ahead. You know you can always tell me everything.

A: 有些事情我想跟你谈谈，但是不知道从何说起。

B: 说吧，你知道你可以对我无话不说。

② **Good luck to you**、祝你好运。使用的场合很广泛，可以是希望对方考试顺利，找到想去的目的地或者其他想要达成的愿望。例如：

A: I'm going to propose to my girlfriend tomorrow.

B: Wow! That's a big news! Good luck to you.

A: 我明天要跟我女朋友求婚。

B: 哇! 这可是重大消息! 祝你好运。

③ **If everything goes right**、如果一切顺利的话。类似表达方式还有**If all goes well**、(缩写为IAGW)，但这是商务英语中的邮件用语，比较简洁。例如：

A: I'll get my driving license in two weeks, if everything goes well.

B: You mean you need to pass the exam?

A: Yeah, you know what I mean.

A: 如果一切顺利的话，再过两周我就可以拿到驾照了。

B: 你是说通过考试以后?

A: 是啊，你懂我的意思。

4 My pleasure、我很荣幸；别客气；非常高兴为您服务。对比 You are welcome. 是更加礼貌的表达方式，当然也相对正式。例如：

A: You have done a wonderful opening speech. Thank you very much, sir.

B: It's my pleasure to speak on this opening ceremony.

　　A：您做了一次非常精彩的开场演讲。非常感谢您，先生。

　　B：在这场开幕式上讲话是我的荣幸。

5 No problem、没问题。在对方询问意见时或者表达感谢之后都可以使用，表示不值得一提，没有什么大不了的。例如：

A: I need to take a quick look in the garden. Can you wait a second?

B: No problem. Go ahead.

　　A：我需要去花园看一下。你能稍等一会儿吗？

　　B：没问题。你去吧。

6 Thanks anyway、依然谢谢你。同义的说法有 Thank you anyway。在对方无法提供你所需要的帮助时，仍然表示感谢，是一种很礼貌的表达方式。例如：

A: Sorry, I don't know where Brussel Street is.

B: No problem. Thank you anyway.

　　A：不好意思，我不知道布鲁塞尔街在哪儿。

　　B：没问题。依然感谢你。

7 You see? 明白了吗? 类似的说法有Is that clear? 或者 Did you get it? 用于在为对方解释之后，询问对方是否明白。例如：

A: This is how the machine starts and works. You see?

B: Absolutely. Thanks for the presentation.

A：这就是这台机器启动和运转的方式。明白了吗?

B：是的，很明白。谢谢你的展示。

表达方式百宝箱

本课中我们学习了用于问方向或问路的不同表达方式，读者朋友们可以在日常使用中变换运用。相应的，回答的信息也尤为重要，是我们找到正确地点的关键。那么，究竟有哪些方式来提问和解答呢，就让我们一起来总结一下吧!

一，问路的表达方式

Can you help me? 你能帮助我吗?

Do you know how to go to Sint-Peter Music School? 你知道去圣彼得音乐学校怎么走吗?

Do you know where the post office is? 你知道邮局在哪儿吗?

Where is Sint-Peter Music School? 圣彼得音乐学校在哪儿?

二，回答

At the end of the street you turn left. 在街尾左转。

Go straight along this street. 沿着这条街直走。

Turn to the first street on the right. 右边第一个路口右转。

You follow this street till the second crossroad, and then turn to the right. 沿着这条街走到第二个十字路口，然后右转。

小丫 带你走遍美国

纽约的华尔街（Wall Street）

华尔街（Wall Street）是纽约市曼哈顿区南部从百老汇路延伸到东河的一条大街道的名字，全长仅500多米，宽仅11米，以"美国的金融中心"而闻名于世。现在，"华尔街"一词已超越这条街道本身，成为附近区域的代称，亦可指对整个美国经济具有影响力的金融市场和金融机构。

早在荷兰殖民者统治时期，在这里筑过一道防卫墙。1664年，英国统治者赶走荷兰殖民者之后，拆除围墙，建起了街道，因此得名"Wall Street"。在世界经济一体化的今天，华尔街已经跨越了国界，扩展到全球的各个角落。所以，真正意义上的华尔街，不仅包括每天在华尔街上忙忙碌碌的几十万人，也包括远在佛罗里达的基金经理、加州"硅谷"的风险投资家或美国投资银行在伦敦的交易员等。事实上，作为美国金融服务业的总称，华尔街实际上已经代表了一个自成体系的金融帝国。2001年9月11日，位于华尔街附近纽约金融区的世界贸易大厦遭到恐怖袭击，纽约交易所停止交易，这一刻，美国经济乃至世界经济几乎停摆。华尔街这个金融帝国的影响力由此可见一斑。

2011年9月17日，上千名示威者聚集在美国纽约曼哈顿，试图占领华尔街，有人甚至带了帐篷，扬言要长期坚持下去。他们通过互联网组织起来，要把华尔街变成埃及的解放广场。示威组织者称，他们的意图是要反对美国政治的权钱交易、两党政争以及社会不公正。2011年10月8日，"占领华尔街"抗议活动呈现升级趋势，千余名示威者在首都华盛顿游行，如今已逐渐成为席卷全美的群众性社会运动。

第17课

姑妈来了

情景介绍: 远离家乡,在异国追逐梦想是每个留学生的真实写照。自然而然,有亲人或朋友来探望是件让人无比兴奋的事。然而"有朋自远方来"真的让人满心欢喜吗?让我们一起来看看小丫姑妈来访的经历吧,就知道这其中的玄机了。

会话1

Ya: This is Ya Jiang. Good morning.

Aunt: Good morning, Ya! This is your aunt. How are you?

Ya: I'm good.

Aunt: I'm coming to America next week.

Ya: Really? Excellent! When are you coming exactly?

Aunt: I'm coming on the twenty-sixth November, in the morning. It's a business trip together with three other colleagues, so I won't have so much time for you.

Ya: That's no problem. It's already good enough just to see you. What day is it that day?

Aunt: It's a Saturday. I take off in Beijing on Friday afternoon.

Ya: Do I need to come and get you in the airport?

Aunt: Yeah, that will be perfect!

Ya: Can you give me a ring when you land, or is it too difficult for you?

Aunt: No no no, that's no problem.

Ya: Ok. I'll go as soon as the phone rings.

Aunt: All right. Then see you this weekend!

Ya: See you.

小丫：我是蒋小丫。早上好。

姑妈：早上好，小丫！我是你姑妈。你怎么样？

小丫：我很好啊。

姑妈：我下周去美国。

小丫：真的吗？太棒了！你具体什么时候来？

姑妈：我是11月26号早上到。这是一次商务旅行，同行的还有另外三个同事，所以可能跟你见面的时间不会太久。

小丫：没问题。能见到你就已经很不错了。26号是星期几？

姑妈：星期六。我周五下午从北京起飞。

小丫：我需要去机场接你吗？

姑妈：那样最好不过了！

小丫：飞机降落时你能给我打个电话吗？或者这对你来说太困难了？

姑妈：不困难，没问题。

小丫：好的，你一给我打电话我就出发去机场。

姑妈：好的。那么就这个周末见！

小丫：周末见。

会话2

Stewardess: Sir, madam, do you want anything to drink?

Neighbor: I'd like a cup of coffee, please.

Aunt: I'd like a cup of tea. Oh, no, I'm feeling like something tasty, so I'll take a glass of red wine. Or perhaps whisky, something strong. A glass of whisky, please.

Stewardess: Here you are, sir. And this is yours, madam.

Neighbor: Thank you.

Aunt: Miss, excuse me. Can I also have a glass of red wine?

Stewardess: No problem, madam. Here you are.

Aunt: Mr, you drink coffee without sugar? Black coffee is not healthy.

Neighbor: Mmm…

空姐：先生，女士，你们要喝点什么吗？

邻座：我要一杯咖啡，谢谢。

姑妈：我要一杯茶。哦，不对，我想要点好喝的，所以还是要一杯红酒吧。或者一杯威士忌，口味重一点。一杯威士忌吧，谢谢。

空姐：给您，先生。给您，女士。

邻座：谢谢。

姑妈：小姐，不好意思。我可以再要一杯红酒吗？

空姐：没问题，女士。给您。

姑妈：先生，你喝咖啡不加糖吗？黑咖啡不健康。

邻座：嗯……

会话3

Aunt:	I don't think night flights are pleasant.
Neighbor:	Excuse me. What did you just say?
Aunt:	I said that I found night flights are not pleasant. In the day, we can see through the window and look at the clouds. But in the night, I don't scc anything. Everything is black, and I can't even sleep here.

Neighbor: Mmm…

Aunt: Do you often travel at night?

Neighbor: Yeah, I think it's ok.

Aunt: Can't be. Really?

Neighbor: Excuse me, but I'm tired, and I'm trying to get some sleep.

Aunt: Sorry.

姑妈： 我觉得夜间飞行真让人不愉快。

邻座： 不好意思，你刚刚说什么？

姑妈： 我说我觉得夜间飞行让人不愉快。在白天，我们可以看着窗外，看看云朵。但是在晚上什么也看不见。外面都是黑色的，我在这儿也睡不着。

邻座： 嗯……

姑妈： 你经常夜里旅行吗？

邻座： 是的，我觉得还不错。

姑妈： 不是吧。真的吗？

邻座： 不好意思，我有点累了。我想睡一会儿。

姑妈： 对不起。

会话4

Ya: This is Ya Jiang. Good morning.

Aunt: Ya, this is your aunt! Are you up, girl?

Ya: Yes…No, but it doesn't matter.

Aunt: I'm now in the airport. Can you come and get me?

Ya: What are you saying? Are you serious? How can it be? It's only Wednesday!

Aunt: You know I like being early.

Ya: Yes, but…

Aunt: Are you coming, or do I need to take a taxi?

Ya: Today I have lessons.

Aunt: Yes, I know. You first come to get me in the airport and then go to your lesson. It's not a big deal.

Ya: Then I'll be too late, and the professor…

Aunt: Don't take me wrong, but only once isn't that bad. I see you later?

Ya: Ok, see you later.

小丫: 我是蒋小丫，早上好。

姑妈: 小丫，我是姑妈！你起床了吗，丫头？

小丫: 起了……哦，还没，不过没关系。

姑妈: 我现在在机场。你能来接我吗？

小丫: 你说什么？是说真的吗？怎么会呢？今天才星期三啊！

姑妈: 你知道的，我喜欢提前。

小丫: 我知道，但是……

姑妈: 你过来吗？还是我要打车？

小丫: 今天我有课啊。

姑妈: 是啊，我知道。你先来机场接我，然后再去上课。没什么大不了的。

小丫：那我就迟到了，而且教授……
姑妈：你别误会，但就这么一次没那么严重。我们一会儿见？
小丫：好吧，一会儿见。

必备词汇

take off v.

起飞，脱下，离开

在本课中意为"飞机起飞"。

例如 This plane always takes off on time. 这架飞机总是按时起飞。

whisky ['hwiski] n.

威士忌酒

例如 Whisky is a strong alcoholic drink. 威士忌是一种烈性的酒精饮料。

neighbor ['neibə] n.

邻居，邻近的人

excellent
['eksələnt] adj.

卓越的，极好的，杰出的

在口语中使用，表示"太棒了，棒极了，太好了！" **例如** That's excellent! I've been waiting for this movie for ages. 太棒了！我等这部电影已经等了太久了。

stewardess
['stjuwə,dis] n.

空姐，服务人员

例如 Being a stewardess is the dream of many young girls. 成为一名空姐是很多年轻女孩的梦想。

pleasant
['pleznt] adj.

令人愉快的，舒适的，讨人喜欢的

例如 Walking in the park is pleasant. 在公园中散步是很令人愉快的。

healthy
['helθi] adj.

健康的，健全的，有益健康的

可以用来形容人，也可以用来形容食物或生活方式等。
例如 Smoking is not healthy. 吸烟不健康。

land
[lænd] v.

着陆，登陆，到达

与take off相对应。**例如** His flight landed 15 minutes late last night. 昨晚他的航班延迟了15分钟着陆。

perhaps
[pə'hæps, præps] adv.

也许，可能

同义词有maybe、possibly和probably。
例如 Perhaps he lost his wallet in the station. 也许他把钱包丢在车站了。

地道美语

1 **Can't be.** 一定不是；不可能。是That can't be true的简单表达方式，表示不相信对方所说的话。例如：

A: My new book is gone. Do you know where it is?

B: Can't be. I just saw it yesterday in the book shelf.

　A：我的新书不见了。你知道它在哪儿吗？

　B：不可能，我昨天还在书架上看见了。

2 **Give me a ring.** 给我打个电话。/给我来个电话。是比较口语化的表达方式，对比Call me语气要轻松愉悦得多。例如：

A: If you have any problem, just give me a ring.

B: Thanks. I'll let you know when I need you.

　A：如果你有任何问题，尽管给我来个电话。

　B：谢谢。如果有需要我会告诉你的。

3 **How are you?/ I'm good.** 你怎么样？/我很好。这是大部分读者在英语入门时就学过的句式了，其实回答"I'm good./ Not bad./ I'm doing ok." 是比较低调的方式。如果再回答"I'm fine."，可能会被对方笑话哦。例如：

A: How are you doing? It's been a long time since we met last time.

B: I'm good. Thanks. How about you?

　A：你怎么样？自从我们上次见面已经很长时间了。

　B：我很好。谢谢。你呢？

4 I'll go as soon as the phone rings. 电话一响我就出发。注意句中as soon as的用法，意为"一……就……"例如：

A: I'll start my trip as soon as the exams are over.
B: That's an excellent idea.

　　A：考试一结束我就开始旅行。
　　B：这个主意太棒了！

5 on Friday afternoon 星期五下午。"在星期五"的英语表达是on Friday，而"在下午"的英语表达是in the afternoon，当二者结合变成在某一天的下午时英语表达用介词on。例如：

A: When are you coming to my apartment?
B: On Sunday morning.

　　A：你什么时候来我的公寓？
　　B：星期天早晨。

6 See you this weekend. 这个周末见。"在周末"的英语表达是in the weekend，但当weekend前面有其他修饰语时，介词省略。例如：

A: Are you free next weekend?
B: Sorry, but I already have an appointment.

　　A：你下周末有空吗？
　　B：对不起，我下周末已经有约了。

另外，类似的表达还有See you tomorrow. / See you next week./ See you on Monday.等等，分别意为"明天见。/下周见。/周一见"。

7 something tasty/ something strong 美味的东西/ 口味重的东西。注意something和形容词的语序，用于修饰something的形容词位于此形容词之后。例如：

A: He doesn't eat anything spicy.

B: It's the opposite to me. I always want something spicy.

A：他不吃任何辣的东西。

B：和我刚好相反。我总是想吃点辣的东西。

8 What day is it? 星期几？day是专门用于问星期几的。如果问"今天是几号？"问题则是What date is it today? 例如：

A: Does anyone know what day it is today?

B: Sure. It's Saturday, so you don't need to work.

A：有人知道今天是星期几吗？

B：当然啦。今天是星期六，所以你不用上班。

表达方式百宝箱

　　本课中小丫的姑妈要来拜访，因此她们在电话中谈论了如何接机。而姑妈并没有像约定中说的周六到，而是提早到达了，小丫表示了惊讶。面对诸多情景，我们还是赶快来把本课的表达方式整理一下吧！

How are you?/ I'm good. 你怎么样？/我很好。

Can't be. 一定不是。／不可能。

Just give me a ring. 给我来个电话。／给我打个电话。

I'll go as soon as the phone rings. 电话一响我就出发。

See you this weekend. 这个周末见。

What day is it? 星期几？

小丫 带你走遍 美国

美国航空（American Airlines）

美国航空公司(American Airlines)，或称美利坚航空公司，简称美航，在载客量和机队大小上是全世界最大的航空公司，也是在营收上第二大的航空公司，仅次于法国航空——荷兰皇家航空集团。它的总部位于得克萨斯州的沃斯堡，紧邻达拉斯——沃斯堡国际机场，执行的航班遍及整个美国，还有飞往加拿大、拉丁美洲、西欧、日本、中国、和印度的航班。

美国航空公司是由大约82家小航空公司组合通过一系列整合和改革发展而来的。最初，许多飞机都可以自由使用American Airways这个名字作为共有品牌。1934年，美国航空公司陷入财政危机，在E·L·Cord的领导下，将公司更名为"American Airlines"。早期的时候，公司的总部位于伊利诺伊州的芝加哥中途机场。在这段时期美航的一个创新就是在飞机上使用了空乘人员。

它拥有美国引以为傲的飞行体验——优质的服务、世界级的娱乐设施，以及有求必应的服务态度。这也是美国航空的独到之处。即使是经济舱航班，也可以享受到收听CD、观看DVD，或者通过便携式电脑上网，或为手机充电等服务。投影屏幕上放映着当前热播的电影、新闻、纪录片，以及喜剧片。在上海到芝加哥的波音777航班上，椅背视频系统可提供10个频道的节目和电影。

在科技高速发展的今天，乘飞机出行成为很多人的首选，不仅节约了时间，也免除了很多旅途的劳顿之苦。

第18课

梦回中国：纽约的唐人街

情景介绍： 几乎在世界上任何国家都能看到勤劳勇敢的中国人的身影，他们有的经营餐厅，有的经营商店。也许他们已经不是第一代移民，然而对于远在他乡的留学生们来说，能看见熟悉的黄皮肤已经很让人欣慰。今天，小丫要带一直对中国文化感兴趣的汤姆和杰瑞去逛逛纽约的唐人街。让我们快去看看吧！

会话1

Jerry: This is Jerry.

Ya: Hello, Jerry. This is Ya. Shall we do an interesting tour in the China Town? You and Tom have always been curious about China.

Jerry: Sure. I'm totally in. Hold on for a second. I'm going to ask Tom, but I'm sure he will say yes too.

Tom: Hey, Ya. Why didn't you call me? Of course, I'm one hundred percent interested. When shall we start?

Ya: We will start now. I'm coming over to you guys, and then we will go there together. How does that sound?

Tom and Jerry: Sounds perfect. See you later.

Ya: See you.

杰瑞：我是杰瑞。

小丫：你好啊，杰瑞，我是小丫。我们今天去"唐人街"转转怎么样？你和汤姆不是一直对中国很感兴趣嘛。

杰瑞：当然好啊。我完全赞成。稍等一下，我去问问汤姆，不过我觉得他也一定会想去的。

汤姆：你好啊，小丫。你怎么没给我打电话呢？我当然百分之百的感兴趣了。我们什么时候出发？

小丫：我们现在就出发。我现在去你们的公寓，然后我们一起走。你们觉得怎么样？

汤姆和杰瑞：好极了，一会儿见。

小丫：一会儿见。

会话2

Tom: It's not the first time for me to be here, but it's truly the first time with a Chinese in the China Town.

Jerry: It's the first time for me, so you can be my full-time guide, Ya.

Ya: It's also the first time for me, and I'm not sure how it will go.

Tom: Ya, you are from Beijing, right?

Ya: Yeah, right. I have been in Beijing since I was born.

Tom: So I guess you probably don't speak Cantonese. I heard many Chinese in the States speak Cantonese instead of Mandarin Chinese.

Ya: Indeed. I know that, too. Some people even speak Hakkas. Most immigrants are from the south of China, and some of them have stayed here ever since.

Tom: How about we eating Peking duck here?

Ya: I'm not sure if it's a good idea. As you know, most people here are from the south of China, but Beijing duck is of course from Beijing.

Jerry: That makes sense, but for people who have never been to China like me and Tom, all Chinese is Chinese. We don't really see the difference between Northern Chinese and Southern Chinese. Some people even don't tell the difference between different Asian countries.

Ya: Yeah, I know what you mean. If you are up for a dinner in China town, we shall try the typical Cantonese food. I'm sure we can get the real thing. By the way, when is this China Town founded?

Tom: Well, it's officially founded in 1890, but in 1851, the population of Chinese immigrants in America was already about 25,000. At the beginning, they took the work that the local people didn't want to do, such as mining, farming and cutting trees.

Ya: I see. Now they know running a restaurant is way better than hard labor.

Tom and Jerry: Haha, right!

汤姆：这不是我第一次来唐人街，但确实是第一次和中国人一起来。

杰瑞：我是第一次来，所以你可以做我的全职导游，小丫。

小丫：我也是第一次来，而且我还不确定这里怎么样呢。

汤姆：小丫，你是北京人，对吗？

小丫：是的，没错。我一出生就住在北京。

汤姆：所以我猜你大概不会讲粤语吧。我听说在美国的很多中国人都说粤语，而不是普通话。

小丫：没错。我也知道。一些人甚至讲客家话。美国的大部分中国移民都是来自中国南方，一些移民从

此就留在了美国。

汤姆： 我们在这儿吃北京烤鸭怎么样？

小丫： 我不确定这是不是一个好主意。你知道的，这儿的大多数人来自中国南方，北京烤鸭呢，自然是来自北京啦。

杰瑞： 有道理。但是对于从没去过中国的人来说，比如我跟汤姆，所有的中国人都是中国人。我们不是很清楚北方人跟南方人的区别。一些人甚至不知道亚洲不同国家之间的区别。

小丫： 是的，我明白你的意思了。如果你们想在唐人街吃饭，我们最好试试广东菜。我确定我们能吃到正宗的。顺便问一下，唐人街是什么时候建立的？

汤姆： 嗯，正式建立是在1890年，但实际是在1851年，在美国的中国移民已经有差不多2.5万人了。开始的时候，他们做着美国人不愿意从事的工作，比如采矿工人、农场工人和伐木工人。

小丫： 我知道了。现在他们意识到开餐馆远远比重劳力好了。

汤姆和杰瑞： 哈哈，你说得对！

必备词汇

Hakkas n.

客家人，客家话

例如 Hakkas has a unique spirit of the Hakka. 客家人具有独特的客家精神。

Cantonese
[ˌkæntəˈniːz] n.

广东人，广东话
adj. 广州的。
例如 Cantonese is commonly spoken in Hong Kong. 在香港，人们通常讲粤语。

curious
[ˈkjuriəs] adj.

好奇的，有求知欲的；古怪的，奇特的
例如 Children are always curious about things around them. 孩子总是对他们周围的事物感到好奇。

found
[faund] v.

创立，建立，创办
例如 The firm has never had an unprofitable year since its founding 65 years ago. 该公司自65年前成立以来从没有过不盈利的年度。

guy
[gai] n.

男人，家伙
常在口语中使用，不限于称呼男性。
例如 I used to work with a guy from New York. 我以前曾和一个纽约人共事过。

full-time adj.

专职的，全日制的，全职的，全部时间的
相对应的有part-time，兼职的，非全职的。例如 Being a mom is a full-time job. 妈妈是一项全职的工作。

Asian
[ˈeiʃən] n.

亚洲人；adj. 亚洲人的，亚洲的
例如 China is the biggest Asian country. 中国是最大的亚洲国家。

immigrant ['imigrənt] n.

移民，侨民；候鸟

例如 Illegal immigrants are getting a serious problem in the US. 非法移民正在成为美国一个严重的问题。

Mandarin Chinese n.

中国官话，普通话

或称为Putonghua，standard Chinese。

例如 All students in China need to learn Mandarin Chinese at school. 在中国所有在校学生都要学习普通话。

Peking duck

北京烤鸭，北京鸭

例如 Many foreigners like to try Peking duck when they go to China. 许多外国人来中国时喜欢试试北京烤鸭。

地道美语

1 Hold on for a second. 稍等一会儿。是在打电话时请对方稍等的表达方式，也可以使用在日常对话中。例如：

A: Do you know how to get to the Park?

B: I think I have the map somewhere. Hold on for a second, I'm going to check.

    A：你知道怎么去公园吗？

    B：我觉得我有地图。稍等一会儿，我看一下。

2 How does that sound? 听起来怎么样？是征求对方意见的表达方式，that指代上文已经出现过的意见、建议或者提议。例如：

A: I propose that I go for a coffee before we say goodbye. How does that sound?

B: It sounds good to me. Let's go for a coffee.

> A：我提议我们在说再见之前去喝杯咖啡。听起来怎么样？
>
> B：我觉得不错，我们去喝杯咖啡吧。

③ That makes sense. 有道理。反义的表达方式是That doesn't make sense. 没道理，没理由。是表示赞同或者不赞同对方意见的表达方式。例如：

A: The reason he failed the final exam is that he didn't study at all.

B: That makes sense. Who can pass the exam without studying?

> A：他期末考试没通过的原因是他根本没学习。
>
> B：有道理。谁能不学习就通过考试呢？

表达方式百宝箱

本课中小丫和汤姆、杰瑞一起去参观了纽约的唐人街，他们的对话中出现了一些中国群体的名词，以及唐人街的建立。那么就让我们来回顾一下相关的表达方式吧。

Hold on for a second. 稍等一会儿。

How does that sound? 听起来怎么样？

That makes sense. 有道理。

小丫 带你走遍 美国

纽约的唐人街——China Town

纽约唐人街位于纽约市曼哈顿南端下城，其范围以勿街为中心，包括坚尼街、摆也街、披露街、拉菲耶特街、包厘街和东百老汇大道。距市政府仅一步之遥，与闻名世界的国际金融中心华尔街也只是咫尺之遥，又毗邻世界表演艺术中心的百老汇，优越的地理位置使它在纽约有着举足轻重的地位。今天的纽约唐人街，已扩展为45条街道，面积超过4平方公里。它已完全吞并了周边的犹太区和波多黎各区、蚕食意大利区。到2007年，纽约的华人已达80万之多，已形成4座中国城和10个华人社区。纽约唐人街的变迁就是一部海外华人发展壮大的历史。

纽约最早的唐人街是在1890年形成的。1848年，两男一女共3位台山人乘坐"流浪之鹰"号帆船到达美国，这是最早移民美国的中国人。到1851年，移入美国西海岸的五区人已达2.5万人，以后逐年增加。这些华侨们在矿场、农场、雪茄厂、木材厂做着美国白人不肯做的工作。1880年美国发生经济危机，白人大批失业，而中国人却有工作做。于是，大批白人开始嫉恨中国人，无端地指责中国人抢了他们的饭碗。由此，加利福尼亚州通过了《排华法案》，被排挤和受迫害的中国人向美国东海岸迁移。首先进入纽约的华人在曼哈顿下城东南区的勿街（Mottstreet，意译丛林街）、柏克街（Parkstreet，意译公园街）落脚，随着人口的逐步增加，1890年唐人街形成。唐人街的英文名称是Chinatown，意译中国城。

纽约唐人街的居民以华人为主，华人的商业活动也集中于此。住在唐人街就像在中国大陆、台湾和香港等其他华人聚居区一样。通用的语言主要是普通话，当然也有各地方言。中餐为主食，许多街口都有中文报摊。开车可以听到中文广播，晚间看的电视是中文电视。在美国，只有唐人街有这样的条件和氛围。同时，华人也在此从事商业活动，主要是开商店、饭店和礼品店。居民的来源地主要是广东和香港，因此主要的语言为粤语。

第19课

租车自驾游

情景介绍: 在美国，开车出行非常方便。有人甚至说，在美国，如果没有车简直寸步难行。如果想要去别的城市，或者别的州，自驾出行无疑是最好的旅行方式。但是，对于留学生和大部分美国本土大学生来说，上学期间有一部自己的车并不是那么简单。租车便成了广受欢迎的方式，方便快捷，而且价格相对低廉。今天，小丫和汤姆及好朋友们就要租车出游，让我们来看看吧。

会话1

Tom: Good morning. Is this Nick Car Rental?

Service person: Right, sir. What can I do for you?

Tom: I want to rent a car.

Service person: Well, you have made the right choice then. We have a wide selection of vehicles you can choose from.

Tom: I would like a car with a good stereo.

Service person: All our cars have stereos in them, installed stereos and air conditioning. It's all standard with us.

Tom: Good. My friends and I are planning to visit the lakes. We want to have a good time.

Service person: Oh, is that so? Well, then. Let me show you something you and your friends might like. By the way, how many people will be there in the car?

Tom: There will be four.

Service person: I see. Take a look at this Ford. It's a car big enough for six people.

Tom: Will it be very expensive?

Service person: Don't worry. It's not expensive at all. It has already some miles, but it still looks new, and all the gears are in a good shape.

Tom: Indeed. I think I'll take this car. I want to buy the insurance too. It's necessary, isn't it?

Service person: Yes, sir. I think it's smart of you to buy it. It's 60 dollars for one week. It's a good ideal, isn't it?

Tom: Can I return the car in Montana?

Service person: Montana? No, sir. We only have this office here. You will have to return it here.

Tom: Really? I thought we can return rental cars in different cities.

Service person: No, sir. That's only with the very big companies. I'm sorry, but this car must be returned to this agency.

Tom: Well, I guess I will have to drive back down then. Hmm. I didn't think of that.

Service person: Do you still want the car, sir?

Tom: Yes, sure. It will be fun, with a few friends. I think we will enjoy the trip.

Service person: Absolutely. It's always fun with friends. We fill out the forms first, and then you will have the keys.

汤姆：早上好。这里是Nick租车吗？

服务人员：对的，先生。我可以为您做些什么？

汤姆：我想租一辆车。

服务人员：好的，那您就来对地方了。我们有很多款车供您选择。

汤姆：我想要一辆有好音响的车。

服务人员：我们的车都有音响，音响和空调都是内置的。这是我们的标准配置。

汤姆：好的。我跟朋友们打算去参观大湖区。我们想有个愉快的旅行。

服务人员：哦，是这样。嗯，那让我来给您展示一辆车，您和您的朋友应该会喜欢。顺便问一下，车里会有几个人呢？

汤姆：一共会有4个人。

服务人员：我知道了。看一看这款福特车。这辆车足够6个人坐的。

汤姆：它会很贵吗？

服务人员：别担心。它一点也不贵。它已经有些公里数了，但是看起来像新车一样，而且所有设备也都状况完好。

汤姆：确实是这样。我想我就租这辆车了。我还想买保险。这是必需的，是不是？

服务人员：好的，先生。我认为您买保险非常明智。一周60美元。这很便宜，对不对？

汤姆：我可以在蒙大拿州还车吗？

服务人员：蒙大拿州？不可以的，先生。我们只在这有办公室。你必须得在这里的办公室还车。

汤姆：真的吗？我以为可以在别的城市还车呢。

服务人员：不是的，先生。只有大公司才可以。我很抱歉，但是必须得在本公司还车。

汤姆：好吧，我想我就必须得再开回来了。嗯，我没考虑到。

服务人员：那您还要这辆车吗，先生？

汤姆：是的，当然要了。和一群朋友在一起应该会很有意思的。我想我们会享受这段旅程。

服务人员：一定会的。和朋友们在一起总是很愉快的时光。我们填完这些表格，然后您就可以拿钥匙了。

必备词汇

air conditioning n.

空调，冷气，通风

相应地，air conditioner n. 空调，空调机，冷气设备。例如 Air conditioning is necessary in a city like Shanghai. 在像上海这样的城市安装空调很有必要。

rent [rent] v.

出租，租用，租借

n. 租金，租赁费，房租。例如 Renting an apartment is normal for new graduates. 租公寓对刚毕业的学生来说很正常。

selection [si'lekʃən] n.

选择，挑选，选集，精选品

例如 This singer published a new album of the best selection. 这位歌手出了一本新专辑，里面收录了精选歌曲。

vehicle ['viːɪkl] n.

车辆，工具；交通工具，运载工具

例如 The red traffic light indicates that every person and vehicle must stop. 红色信号灯表示人和车辆不能通行。

stereo ['steri,əu, 'stiər-,] n.

立体声，立体声系统，音响设备

stereo system n. 立体声音响系统。例如 My father loved his stereo so much that he would never let me touch it. 我爸爸太喜欢他的立体声音响器材了，他从来都不会让我碰它。

补充词汇

　　本课学习租车的对话，那么跟车有关的词汇大家是不是都熟悉呢？我们一起来总结和复习一下吧。

车的类型：

ambulance n. 救护车　　　　Ford n. 福特汽车

jeep n. 吉普车　　　　　　　racing car n. 赛车

sports car n. 跑车　　　　　truck n. 卡车

taxi n. 出租车，计程车

GPS 全球定位系统，是Global Positioning System的简称。

车内装置：

back seat/ rear seat n. 后座　　dashboard n. 仪表板

first gear n. 一档　　　　　　speedometer/ clock n. 速度表

horn/ hooter n. 喇叭　　　　　milometer n. 里程表

passenger seat n. 旅客席　　　rear wheel n. 后轮

rear window n. 后窗玻璃　　　reverse n. 倒车挡

second gear n. 二挡　　　　　spare wheel n. 备胎，备用轮胎

front wheel n. 前轮　　　　　steering wheel/ wheel n. 方向盘

license plate/ number plate n. 车号牌

windscreen/ windshield n. 挡风玻璃

driver's seat/ driving seat n. 驾驶席

fender/ wing/ mudguard n. 挡泥板

windscreen wiper/ windshield wiper n. 风挡刮水器，风挡雨雪刷

地道美语

1 I didn't think of that. 我没考虑到。也可以表达为I didn't think of it. it或that指代上文出现过的情况。例如：

A: Why did you tell her about the new girl friend of her ex-boyfriend? She's not over him yet, so now she's very sad.

B: I'm sorry, but I didn't think of it.

　A: 你为什么告诉她关于她前男友现任女友的事？她还没放下他呢，所以她现在很伤心。

　B: 对不起，我没考虑到这一点。

例句中出现了She's not over him yet. 和前面学过的She's not very into him. 刚好相反，前者译为：她还没放下他。意为"她心里面还想着他"。后者译为：她并没有很喜欢他。

2 Sunday driver/ Dead legs. 驾车不熟练的驾驶员，开慢车的人。两个短语分别直译为"周日车手"和"死腿"，引申为"开车很慢"。例如：

A: She's really a Sunday driver. I don't know how you can go out with her.

B: I don't have a car, so it's good enough for me to get a free ride.

　A: 她开车真的很慢。我不知道你怎么能忍受和她一起出去。

B: 我没有车，所以有免费的车坐对我来说已经足够好了。

③ **The fifth wheel.** 多余的东西。直译为"第五个车轮"，引申意为"多余的东西，不需要的东西"。例如：

A: I'm tired of being treated like the fifth wheel around here.

B: Hey, don't think like that. Nobody is treating you like a fifth wheel.

A: 我已经厌倦了在这儿被当作多余的人。

B: 嗨，别这样想。没人把你当作多余的人。

④ **You have made the right choice.** 你做出了正确的选择。在本课中译为"你是来对地方了"。是对对方意见、做法、决定或选择给予肯定的表达方式。而具体的译法还要依文中对话的情景来判断。例如：

A: I went to the hair dresser at the corner of the street this time. I think it's better than the one I used to go to.

B: You've made the right choice. I personally think that's the best hair dresser in town.

A: 我这次去了街角的那家理发店。我觉得比我以前常去的理发店要好。

B: 你是去对地方了。我个人认为那是市内最好的理发店。

注意例句中出现了hair dresser n.理发师，理发店。personally adv.亲自地，就自己而言。例如：The Prime Minister answered all the letters personally.总理亲自回复了所有的来信。

表达方式百宝箱

本课中我们学习了租车对话用语，在补充词汇中学习了很多有关车的类型和车内装置的词与词组，希望读者朋友们多多复习。下面让我们一起总结一下有关车的表达方式。

I didn't think of that. 我没考虑到。

Sunday driver/ Dead legs. 驾车不熟练的驾驶员。／开慢车的人。

The fifth wheel. 多余的东西。

You have made the right choice. 你的选择是正确的。

小丫带你走遍美国

福特汽车——Ford Motor

福特汽车公司是世界最大的汽车企业之一。1903年由亨利·福特先生创立创办于美国底特律市。现在的福特汽车公司是世界上的超级跨国公司，总部设在美国密执安州迪尔伯恩市。福特汽车的标志是采用福特英文Ford字样，蓝底白字。

1908年福特汽车公司生产出世界上第一辆属于普通百姓的汽车——T型车，世界汽车工业革命就此开始。1913

年，福特汽车公司又开发出了世界上第一条流水线，这一创举使T型车一共达到了1,500万辆，缔造了一个至今仍未被打破的世界记录。福特先生为此被尊为"为世界装上轮子"的人。在1999年，《财富》杂志将他评为"二十世纪商业巨人"以表彰他和福特汽车公司对人类工业发展所做出的杰出贡献。亨利·福特先生成功的秘诀只有一个：尽力了解人们内心的需求，用最好的材料，由最好的员工，为大众制造人人都买得起的好车。

福特的产品种类繁多。轿车方面有以经济多用性著称的Ka、嘉年华和雅士，有林肯·城市那样宽敞舒适的大型轿车，也有像阿斯顿·马丁和美洲豹之类的华贵汽车。大众化的中级轿车有在澳大利亚生产的猎鹰，在北美生产的特使和黑貂，还有如蒙迪欧、康拓和水星环宇那样的世界级汽车。福特旗下还拥有美洲豹汽车公司、阿斯顿·马丁·拉贡达公司（Aston Martin Lagonea Ltd），并拥有马自达33.4%的股份和起亚汽车公司近10%的股份。福特在世界各地30多个国家拥有生产、总装或销售企业。福特卡车与轿车的销售网遍及6大洲、200多个国家，经销商超过10500家。福特的企业和员工形成了国际网络，在世界各地从事生产、试验、研究、开发与办公的福特员工超过了37万人。

福特汽车公司是世界上第四大工业企业和第二大小汽车和卡车生产商，大约在全世界有36万名职工服务于汽车、农业、金融和通信领域。福特公司的多样化经营范围分别包括电子、玻璃、塑料、汽车零部件、空间技术、卫星通信、国防工程、地基开发、设备租赁和汽车出租。它有三个战略经营单位——汽车集团、多样化产品集团和金融服务（财务公司）。

第20课

庆祝圣诞节

情景介绍： 圣诞节像中国的春节一样，是西方国家最重要的节日。随着全球一体化的发展，很多中国人也开始庆祝圣诞节。那么圣诞节的内涵究竟是什么呢？在节日期间的庆祝方式又有哪些呢？今天就让我们跟着小丫一起来全面了解一下圣诞节，为圣诞节的到来而做准备吧！

会话1

Jerry: Merry Christmas, Ya!

Ya: Merry Christmas! Hey, what plans do you have for this special day?

Jerry: No special plans. I'll have supper with my girlfriend and go to visit her parents. How about you?

Ya: I'm going to the church with Tom first and then go to a Christmas party. Would you and Jessica like to come?

Jerry: I don't know yet. I'll ask Jessica. If we can make it, we will definitely go. Thank you.

杰瑞：圣诞快乐，小丫！

小丫：圣诞快乐！喂，这么特别的日子，你打算怎么庆祝啊？

杰瑞：也没什么打算。我跟女朋友一起吃晚饭，然后我们去拜访她的父母。你呢？

小丫：我先跟汤姆去教堂，然后一起去参加一个圣诞晚会。你和杰西卡想一起来吗？

杰瑞：我还不知道，要问问杰西卡。如果我们能去，我们一定会去的。谢谢你。

会话2

James: Merry Christmas, Ya!

Ya: Merry Christmas!

James: Is it your first Christmas in the States?

Ya: Yes, it is. Hopefully I can see how American people celebrate Christmas.

James: Are you doing anything special?

Ya: Actually my friend is taking me to the church, and then we will go to a Christmas party. What are you doing?

James: Oh, I'm just going to take it easy. I've been very stressed in the last few weeks.

Ya: Right. You can take a break this week. You are not going home?

James: Sure. But I'm not going to parties.

詹姆斯: 圣诞快乐，小丫!

小丫: 圣诞快乐!

詹姆斯: 这是你第一次在美国过圣诞节吗?

小丫: 是啊，希望我能看看美国人是怎么庆祝圣诞节的。

詹姆斯: 你有什么特别的打算吗?

小丫: 实际上，我的一个朋友要带我去教堂，然后我们一起去一个圣诞晚会。你有些什么打算呢?

詹姆斯: 哦，我只想放松一下自己。最近这几周压力太大了。

小丫: 是啊，这周你可以好好休息。你不回家吗?

詹姆斯: 当然回家了。但是我不会去参加晚会。

会话3

Ya: Hey Linda, merry Christmas!

Linda: Merry Christmas, Ya!

Ya: We are having a small pre-party here. You want to have some drinks with us?

Linda: No, thank you. I'm going to get ready for the parade. I have a great costume. Then later today, I'm going to church. If you want, I can give you a costume and you can join the parade, too. It'll be fun. You should come.

Ya: Wow! It sounds fun! I've seen many parades on TV, but I haven't been to one yet.

Linda: Then you definitely should join us.

Ya: Yes, I'll come. Let's go grab a drink first.

小丫：　嗨，琳达，圣诞快乐！

琳达：　圣诞快乐，小丫！

小丫：　我们正在办一个节前小型晚会。你要来和我们一起喝点什么吗？

琳达： 不去了，谢谢。我得为今天的花车游行做准备。我有一身非常漂亮的节日服装呢。然后，我去教堂。如果你愿意的话，我可以给你一身节日服装，这样你就能加入到游行的队伍里了。非常有意思的，你应该来。

小丫： 哇，听起来很有意思！我在电视上看过很多游行，但还从来没参加过呢。

琳达： 那你更应该来加入我们了。

小丫： 好的，我也来。让我们先去喝点什么。

会话4

Ya: There seems to be so much Christmas history.

Tom: Yeah, it has a long history, and the culture of Christmas has changed over the years.

Ya: I don't know when I'll ever remember all of it. Why do you celebrate Christmas?

Tom: Well, Christmas Day, which is 25 December, celebrates the birth of Jesus Christ, the founder of the Christian religion. This is the biggest and best-loved holiday in the US.

Ya: I see. I've read a little about Christianity before. How do you celebrate Christmas in the United States?

Tom: Like the Spring Festival, Christmas is the most important holiday to us. It's a day of family reunion. Every family will have a Christmas tree, decorated with lights, ribbons and other little things. We will put the presents under the tree, and all the family exchange presents. Parents

usually tell their children to put a sock at the bed, and Santa Clause will come down the chimney and put the presents in their socks. But you know, only good children get the presents.

Ya: Children believe it?

Tom: Of course they do. All childen try to behave their best, so they can get the presents from Santa. I used to do the same thing.

Ya: That's interesting. Why do people go to church?

Tom: You know, first of all, Christmas is to celebrate the birth of Jesus, and church is the perfect place where you get the teachings and thoughts of Christianity. It's mostly Christians who go to church. There will be services in the church on special occasions.

Ya: Like a Mass?

Tom: Right.

小丫： 好像有关圣诞节的历史很悠久。

汤姆： 是啊，圣诞节有很长的历史，而且圣诞节的文化这些年来也改变了很多。

小丫： 不知道我什么时候才能记住有关圣诞节的所有历史及变迁。你们为什么庆祝圣诞节呢？

汤姆：　是这样的，圣诞节也就是12月25日，是为了庆祝耶稣基督的出生。他是基督教的创始人。圣诞节是美国最大也是最受欢迎的节日。

小丫：　是这样。我以前读过一点有关基督教的书籍。在美国你们怎么庆祝圣诞节呢？

汤姆：　像中国的春节一样，圣诞节是我们最重要的节日。这是家庭团聚的日子。每个家庭都有一棵圣诞树，装饰有彩灯、缎带和其他的小东西。我们把圣诞礼物放在树下，全家人都交换礼物。父母会告诉孩子把袜子放在床边，圣诞老人会从烟囱爬下来把礼物放进孩子们的袜子里。但是你知道的，只有好孩子才能得到礼物。

小丫：　孩子们相信这个故事吗？

汤姆：　当然相信了。所有的孩子都努力表现得最好，这样他们才能得到圣诞老人的礼物。我以前也是这样。

小丫：　很有意思。人们为什么去教堂？

汤姆：　你知道吗，首先，圣诞节是为了庆祝耶稣的诞生，而且教堂是学习基督教的教义和思想的最完美的地方。大多数去教堂的人都是基督徒。在特殊日子和场合，教堂都会有仪式。

小丫：　像弥撒这样？

汤姆：　是的。

必备词汇

Santa Clause n.

圣诞老人

简称为Santa。

例如 During Christmas, all the children want the presents from Santa Clause. 圣诞节期间，孩子们都想得到圣诞老人的礼物。

reunion
[riˈjuːnjən] n.

重聚，聚会，团圆

例如 The association holds an annual reunion. 这个协会每年举办一次聚会。

Christmas
[ˈkrisməs] n.

圣诞节

例如 Christmas is the most important holiday in western countries. 圣诞节是西方国家最重要的节日。

church
[tʃəːtʃ] n.

教堂，礼拜，教派

例如 New couples like to have their marriage in the church. 新婚夫妇喜欢在教堂举行婚礼。

costume
[ˈkɔstjuːm] n.

服装，装束，戏服，剧装

例如 People dress up in costumes and join the parade in big holidays. 在重大节日，人们穿上特殊服装参加游行。

grab
[græb] v.

抓取，抢夺

例如 If you want to grab their attention, you need to do some more work. 如果你想抓住他们的注意力，那么你要更努力才行。

ribbon
[ˈribən] n.

带，缎带，丝带，带状物

常见的"剪裁"英语为"cut the ribbon"。

例如 The red ribbon doesn't match with my new hat which I bought yesterday. 这条红色的丝带和我昨天买的新帽子不搭。

Christian
['kristjən; -tʃən] n.

基督徒信徒；adj. 基督教的；信基督教的
Christianity [ˌkristi'ænəti] n. 基督教；
基督教精神，基督教教义。

merry
['meri] adj.

愉快的，欢乐的
一般搭配Merry Christmas一起使用，意为
"圣诞快乐"，单词本身很少单独使用。

parade
[pə'reid] n.

游行，阅兵，行进，阅兵场
例如 We have a military parade on the
National Day. 我们在国庆节当天有阅兵
仪式。

religion
[ri'lidʒən] n.

宗教，宗教信仰
是基督教、佛教、印度教等各种宗教的
总称。例如 He doesn't believe in any
religion. 他不相信任何宗教。

stressed
[strest] adj.

紧张的，感到有压力的
例如 He's getting more stressed than
ever because of the new project. 因为新
项目，他正感到前所未有的紧张。

地道美语

1 Are you doing anything special? 你有什么特别的打算吗？
此问句相当于Do you have any special plans?但相比来说更
加口语化。例如：

A: Hey, do you have anything special for the coming weekend?

B: Actually I do. My girlfriend is coming from Canada. I'm going to give her a surprise.

A: 嗨，对即将到来的周末你有什么特别的打算吗？

B: 我还真有。我女朋友要从加拿大过来，我想给她一个惊喜。

② I'm just going to take it easy. 我就是放松一下。take it easy我们已经在前面的课文中学过了，意为"慢慢来，别紧张"。在这句话中意为放松一下。例如：

A: What are you doing for the big party?

B: I think I'm going to take it easy. You guys have fun.

A: 对于那场盛大的聚会你有什么打算？

B: 我觉得我就是放松一下吧。你们好好玩。

③ Join the parade. 学时髦，跟着大众行动。是美式英语的口语表达方式。类似汉语中的"随大流，赶时髦"。例如：

A: All my neighbors have bought new cars, so I also joined the parade.

B: What car did you buy?

A: 我所有的邻居都买了新车，所以我也要随大流。

B: 你买了什么车？

例句中虽然没有明确说明A买了新车，但他用了join the parade表示自己也加入了邻居换车的行列，因此我们知道他也买了新车。

4 Let's go to grab a drink. 让我们先去喝一杯。这里不一定指酒精类饮料，可以是任何饮料。类似的表达方式还有Grab a bite、吃点东西，随便吃几口，先吃点东西垫垫肚子。这是美国年轻人口语中经常使用的句式。例如：

A: When shall we start for the presentation?

B: Let's go to grab a bite first. We can't work with an empty stomach.

    A：我们什么时候开始准备展示？

    B：让我们先去吃点东西，总不能空着肚子开工。

5 Merry Christmas、圣诞快乐。是固定用法，类似的固定用法还有Happy Birthday和Happy New Year、不可以说成Happy Christmas或者Merry New Year。

表达方式百宝箱

    本课中我们学习了有关圣诞节，圣诞节的历史以及如何表示祝贺的表达方式，同时也进行了一些对话练习。现在就让我们一起总结一下吧！

Merry Christmas. 圣诞快乐。

Are you doing anything special? 你有什么特别的打算吗？

I'm just going to take it easy. 我就是放松一下。

Join the parade. 赶时髦，跟着大众行动。

Let's go to grab a drink. 让我们先去喝一杯。

小Y带你走遍美国

圣诞节——Christmas

    圣诞节，也称为耶诞节，是教会年历的一个传统节日，它是基督徒庆祝耶稣基督降生的庆祝日。在圣诞节，

大部分的基督公教（惯称为天主教）教堂都会先在12月24日的圣诞夜，即12月25日凌晨举行子夜弥撒，而部分基督新教（惯称为基督教）派别也会举行子夜敬拜，此两大基督教分支均会在圣诞夜有报佳音活动，然后在12月25日庆祝圣诞节。

根据基督教的福音书，耶稣是圣母玛利亚受圣神（又译圣灵）感孕后在伯利恒生下的，玛利亚和丈夫约瑟当时正在去罗马人口普查注册的路上。耶稣的降生在信徒看来是犹太教预言中的默西亚（即弥赛亚）将要到来计划的实现，因为伯利恒是约瑟祖先大卫一族的家。圣诞节也是西方世界以及其他很多国家和地区的公共假日，圣经实际上并无记载耶稣诞生日期，圣诞节是后人公定的。

圣诞节的英语为Christmas，即"基督弥撒"。有时又缩写为"Xmas"。圣诞习俗数量众多，国与国之间差别很大。大部分人熟悉的圣诞符号及活动，如圣诞树、圣诞火鸡、圣诞柴、冬青、槲寄生以及互赠礼物，都是基督教传教士从早期异教的冬至假日里吸收而来。对冬至的庆祝早在基督教到达北欧之前就在那里广为进行了，今天圣诞节一词在斯堪的纳维亚语里依然是异教的jul（或yule）。圣诞树被认为最早出现在德国。

圣诞节送礼物已经接近成为一个全球通行的习惯了。神秘人物带给小孩子们礼物的概念衍生自圣尼古拉斯，尼古拉斯是一位在四世纪生活在小亚细亚的好心主教。在北美洲，英国殖民者把这一传统融入圣诞假期的庆祝里，而Sinterklaas也就相应的称为圣诞老人或者称为Saint Nick（圣尼克）的人物了。在英籍美国人的传统中，圣诞老人总是快活地在圣诞前夜乘着驯鹿拉的雪橇到来，从烟囱爬进屋内，留下给孩子们的礼物，吃掉孩子们为他留下的食物。他在一年中的其他时间里忙于制作礼物和监督孩子们的行为并记录下来。在美国，孩子们于圣诞夜在壁炉上悬挂圣诞袜，因为圣诞老人说过要在圣诞前夜从烟囱下来把礼物放到袜子里。赠送礼物不单单是指圣诞老人，家庭成员和朋友也互相赠予礼物。

第21课

去汤姆家做客

情景介绍: 去朋友家拜访在中国和其他国家都是很正常的社交活动。那么在美国去朋友家做客时需要送些什么礼物，或者有什么需要注意的礼仪呢? 今天，小丫要去汤姆家做客，我们一起看看小丫是怎么做的吧。

会话1

Ya: What presents do you give when you go to visit friends or other people?

Tom: Well, it depends on the relationship between you and the host.

Ya: What would you do if you visit Jerry's parents, for instance?

Tom: Jerry and I are good friends, so we are pretty close. If I visit his parents, I would take small things like a bunch of flowers for the living room, a magazine for his dad or a pie.

Ya: I see. Do you give wine or chocolate sometimes?

Tom: Normally no wine, maybe chocolate sometimes. It's also up to the preference of the people you visit.

Ya: In China, we mostly give fruits or drinks.

Tom: In the States, we think fruits are for patients.

Ya: That's different.

小丫： 你们去拜访朋友或者其他人时会送什么礼物呢？

汤姆： 嗯，这要取决于你和主人的关系。

小丫： 比如，你去拜访杰瑞的父母会怎么做呢？

汤姆： 杰瑞和我是好朋友，所以我们的关系比较近。如果我去拜访他的父母，我可能会送些小东西，比如放在客厅的一束花，给他爸爸一本杂志或者是一个派。

小丫： 我知道了。你们有时也送酒或者巧克力吗？

汤姆： 一般不送酒，巧克力有可能。也要取决于主人喜欢什么。

小丫： 在中国，我们大多送水果或饮品。

汤姆： 在美国，我们觉得水果是给病人的。

小丫： 哦，这点不一样。

会话2

Ya: I can't wait to see your parents and your home.

Tom: They are very nice people, and they are also interested in China and Chinese culture.

Ya: I've bought some flowers and a box of chocolate.

Tom: It's very nice of you. I'm sure they will appreciate it very much.

Parents: Welcome, Ya! Come on in. We are so glad you could come.

Ya: Thank you for inviting me.

Parents: We have heard so much about you from Tom. Please make yourself at home.

Ya: Here are some flowers for your lovely house.

Mom: It's so nice of you. I'll put them in the living room. Please have a seat. Would you like something to drink?

Ya: I'd like some water. Thank you.

Tom: Ya's from Beijing. You have been interested in China, so now you can ask all the things you want to know.

Dad: No hurry. We have plenty of time to talk about that. Your mom and I have planned a nice dinner with traditional American food. Hopefully Ya will like it.

Ya: I'm sure I will. I like American food quite much. Can I help in the kitchen?

Mom: No no, you stay here. I have prepared the meal. How about Tom giving you a tour of the house?

Ya: That will be very nice.

小丫： 我已经迫不及待要拜访你的父母跟你们家了。

汤姆： 他们都是很友善的人，而且他们也对中国和中国文化很感兴趣。

小丫： 我买了一些花和一些巧克力。

汤姆： 你真是太客气了。我相信他们对此会很感激的。

父母： 欢迎你，小丫。快进来。我们很高兴你能来。

小丫： 谢谢你们邀请我来。

父母： 汤姆经常跟我们谈起你。在这儿就像在自己家里一样。

小丫： 这些花刚好配你们漂亮的房子。

妈妈： 你真客气。我把这些花放在客厅里。请坐。你想喝点什么吗？

小丫： 我喝点水吧，谢谢。

汤姆： 小丫是北京人。你们不是一直对中国很感兴趣嘛，所以你们现在可以问那些你们感兴趣的问题了。

爸爸： 不着急。我们有很多时间来谈论这个话题。你妈妈跟我计划了一顿很好的晚餐，我们吃传统美国菜。希望小丫能够喜欢。

小丫： 我相信我会喜欢的。我很喜欢美国菜。我可以帮忙准备吗？

妈妈： 不用，不用，你就在那儿吧。我已经做了些准备。为什么不让汤姆给你展示一下我们的家呢？

小丫： 那真是太好了。

必备词汇

appreciate [ə'priːʃieit] v.

欣赏，感激，领会，鉴别

用于表示对对方的话或做法的肯定、感激等积极情感。**例如** He really appreciates what the professor has done for him. 他真的很感激教授为他所做的事。

bunch ['bʌntʃ] n.

群，串，束，花束

a bunch of flowers 一束花；a bunch of grapes 一串葡萄。**例如** He's the worst of the bunch. 他是这群朋友中最糟的。

host [həust] n.

主人，主持人，宿主

host country 东道国，主办国，所在国。host city 主办城市，举办城市。**例如** Shanghai was the host city of the last EXPO. 上海是上届世界博览会的主办城市。

living room n.

客厅，起居室

例如 There is a baby bed in their living room, because their house is not that big. 他们的客厅里有一个婴儿床，因为他们的房子不是很大。

lovely ['lʌvli] adj.

可爱的，好看的，令人愉快的

可以用来形容人或者物体。**例如** His sister is a very lovely girl. 他的妹妹是个很可爱的女孩。

patient
[ˌpeiʃənt] n.

病人，患者

adj.有耐心的，能容忍的。

例如 The doctor doubted whether the patient would live through that month. 医生不确定这个病人是否能活过那个月。

preference
['prefərəns] n.

偏好，倾向，优先权

例如 I have no preference for nationalities. 我对国籍没有特殊偏好。

for instance

例如，比如，举例来说

同义说法有for example。在学过这种说法之后大家就可以替换使用了。

wine
[wain] n.

酒，葡萄酒，酒红色

主要指西方国家的葡萄酒，分为red wine和white wine，分别意为"红葡萄酒"和"白葡萄酒"。

地道美语

1. Can I help in the kitchen? 我可以帮忙准备饭菜吗？去别人家做客时，如果主人邀请客人一起吃饭，客人可以礼貌地问需不需要帮忙，当然，大部分时候除了亲属和非常亲近的朋友之外，主人一般都不会让客人帮忙的。例如：

A: Hey, sis, do I need to help in the kitchen?
B: Yeah, that will be good. Can you wash the tomatoes for me?

A: 嗨，姐姐，需不需要我来厨房帮你？

B: 好啊，当然好了。你能帮我洗洗西红柿吗？

例句中，因为出现了sis，这是sister的简称，可见对话双方是比较亲密的关系。对话中常出现名字的简称，比如Mel是Meliney的简称，Lis是Elisabeth的简称，Nick是Nicolas的简称等。

---

② **I can't wait to see your parents、我迫不及待想拜访你的父母。can't wait to do sth意为"迫不及待要做某事"。表示说话人想做某事的急切心情。例如：**

A: I can't wait to hear your date yesterday.

B: Well, it was OK, not as great as you are expecting.

A: 我迫不及待想听听你昨天的约会。

B: 嗯，其实还可以，没有你想象得那么好。

---

③ **No hurry、不着急。可以出现在对话中，表示"不必着急，慢慢来"。或者出现在文本中，表示一种不紧不慢的状态。例如：**

A: We'll be late. Can't you drive faster?

B: No hurry. Safety comes first.

A: 我们就要迟到了，你不能开快点儿吗？

B: 不着急。安全第一。

---

④ **Please make yourself at home、让自己舒服点。/就像在自己家里一样。这是主人对来访客人说的客气话，表示让客人不要拘谨。例如：**

A: Your house is so beautiful.

B: Thank you. Please make yourself at home.

A：你们的房子真漂亮。

B：谢谢。就像在你自己家里一样。

5 Thank you for inviting me. 谢谢你邀请我来。去别人家拜访，应该礼貌地感谢主人的邀请。主人可能会礼貌地回答说，"It's our pleasure to have you." 例如：

A: Thank you for inviting me.

B: We are so glad you can come. It's our pleasure to have you.

A：谢谢你们邀请我。

B：我们很高兴你能来，这是我们的荣幸。

6 We are so glad you could come. 我们很高兴你能来。是主人表示对客人欢迎的礼貌用语。去别人家做客时，主人和客人之间的礼节性对话是不可避免的。例如：

A: We are so glad you could come.

B: I have been thinking to visit you guys for a long time.

A：我们真高兴你能来。

B：我想来你们家做客已经有一段时间了。

7 Would you like something to drink? 你想喝点什么吗？一般去别人家做客，在客人落座之后，主人会先问客人要不要喝点什么。这时，客人只要如实回答即可。即使不渴，也最好礼貌地索要一杯简单的饮料。例如：

A: Would you like something to drink? We've got tea, coffee, juice, beer and water.

B: Tea will be good for me. Thank you.

A：你想喝点什么吗？我们有茶、咖啡、果汁、啤酒和水。

B：喝茶比较好。谢谢。

表达方式百宝箱

本课中我们学习了去别人家做客时的礼貌用语，也了解了去做客时可以送哪些礼物、怎样对主人及主人的家表示赞美。现在就让我们一起来总结一下吧。

Can I help in the kitchen? 我可以帮忙准备饭菜吗？

I can't wait to see your parents. 我迫不及待想拜访你的父母。

No hurry. 不着急。

Please make yourself at home. 让自己舒服点；就像在自己家里一样。

Thank you for inviting me. 谢谢你们邀请我。

We are so glad you could come. 我们很高兴你能来。

Would you like something to drink? 你想喝点什么吗？

小丫带你走遍美国

去美国家庭做客

约会要周到，赴约要守时，做客时更要彬彬有礼、自然大方。首先要敲门或按门铃，得到主人允许之后才进门。有些人家门口放有擦鞋的棕毡。就应该把鞋上的泥土擦干净，以免弄脏主人的地毯。戴帽子的人进门后要摘帽，在房间里戴着帽子是很不礼貌的。如果是雨天走访，应该注意把雨伞、雨衣放在室外。大衣、外套脱下后，主人一般会主动接过去挂起来，这时可以不必客气。进屋

后，要先向女主人问好，此后向男主人问好。如遇主人家还有其他客人，那么只需同主人和相识者握手，对其他人点头致意即可。

在美国人家中做客，不必过分拘礼。如果主人请你就座，你为了表示客气而不马上坐下，反而会使主人感到不安，以为椅子上不洁或有其他不便。做客时不可随意观看主人桌上的字纸或翻阅文件。不要摆弄室内的古董珍玩，更不要询问室内用具的价格。做客时，不要轻易吸烟。如果想吸烟，应该首先问在座的女士们是否介意，并先向其他人敬烟。如果主人主动请你吸烟，那么即使自己有烟，也要接受主人的烟，而不可拒绝对方而吸自己的烟。否则，主人会认为你是看不起他而感到很不愉快。

中国人请客吃饭时，往往是自谦地表示饭菜做得不好，请客人多多包涵。而美国人却要说"这是我最拿手的菜，希望你们喜欢吃"一类的话。所以，在美国人家中做客，听到主人自夸饭菜做得好，不必奇怪，应对女主人的手艺夸赞几句。中国的主人为客人夹菜时，客人总是尽力推让，表示客气。在美国这样做是行不通的。主人第一次为你夹菜，你不必客气推让，否则女主人会以为你是嫌她的菜做得不好。在餐桌上，女主人是无形中的首脑人物。上菜之后，客人一般要待女主人动手吃后才开始吃。饭后也应由女主人领头离席客人才离席。

在美国人家中做客的时间不宜太长，以免耽搁主人过多的时间。但饭后不要立即告辞，应再和主人攀谈一会儿，然后道谢离去。如果是夫妇一同到别人家去做客，应由妻子先起立告辞。在比较正式的宴会上，如果客人较多，应等年长位高的宾客或重要的女宾先告辞后，自己才告辞。如果客人有事需要先走，应向主人请求原谅后再离去。如果你与主人不很熟，那么做客后还应给主人打个电话表示谢意，或者写一张"谢谢您"的短柬寄给主人，这样在礼貌上就更为周全了。

第22课

游迪士尼乐园

情景介绍： 对于大多数来美国的游客来说，迪士尼是绝对不能错过的一站。尤其对童心未泯的年轻人来说，能和迪士尼乐园里的童话人物亲密接触简直就是梦想变成现实。小丫来美国这么久，还没去梦寐以求的迪士尼乐园玩过，这样的遗憾当然要尽快弥补喽。

会话1

Ya: I've been dreaming to go to Disneyland. Do you have time to come with me?

Tom: Sure. I've only been there once when I was a kid.

Ya: How many Disneylands are there in the States?

Tom: There are two in the States, Anaheim and Florida.

Ya: I read that the name Disneyland was changed to Disneyland Park in 1998.

Tom: Right, to distinguish it from the larger Disneyland Resort complex.

Ya: They all belong to The Walt Disney Company.

Tom: Impressive. You know so much about Disney.

Ya: Interest is the best teacher, right?

Tom: Absolutely. Do you know how Walt Disney was inspired?

Ya: Not really. How?

Tom: He came up with the concept of Disneyland after visiting various amusement parks with his daughters in the 1930s and 1940s. So He initially envisioned building a tourist attraction adjacent to his studios in Burbank to entertain fans who wished to visit, but he soon realized that the proposed site was too small. Walt bought a 160-acre site near Anaheim in 1953. Disney California Adventure Park was built on the site of Disneyland's original parking lot and opened in 2001.

Ya: Wow. Now I see.

小丫： 我一直梦想去迪士尼乐园，你有时间和我一起去吗？

汤姆： 当然有了。我只有很小的时候去过一次。

小丫： 在美国有几个迪士尼乐园？

汤姆： 在美国有两个，一个在阿纳海姆，一个在佛罗里达州。

小丫： 我在书上看到说迪士尼乐园在1998年改名为迪士尼主题公园。

汤姆： 是的，是为了避免和迪士尼度假山庄混淆。

小丫： 它们都属于沃特·迪士尼公司。

汤姆： 真了不起。你知道这么多关于迪士尼乐园的事。

小丫： 兴趣是最好的老师，不是吗？

汤姆： 千真万确。你知道沃特·迪士尼是怎样受到启发的吗？

小丫： 还真不知道。怎么受到启发的？

汤姆： 早在20世纪三四十年代，他带女儿游览众多主题公园的时候就有了建造迪士尼乐园的想法。所以他首先在他伯班克的工作室旁边建起了一个旅游景点，以便感兴趣的人参观。但是他很快就注意到场地太小了，于是，沃特1953年在阿纳海姆购置了一块160公顷的土地。迪士尼加州探险乐园是在原迪士尼乐园的停车场旧址上建造起来的，并于2001年开放。

小丫： 哇，现在我知道了。

会话2

Ya: What can we see and do in Disneyland?

Tom: Well, there are a whole lot of things that we can do. They have a lot of live entertainment.

Ya: Oh really? What are the entertainments?

Tom: Many Disney characters can be found throughout the park, greeting visitors, interacting with children, and posing for photos.

Ya: So I can take pictures with Mikey and Minnie!

Tom: Absolutely. There are daily ceremonies as well.

Ya: What kind of ceremonies?

Tom: Every evening at dusk, there is a military-style flag retreat to lower the Flag of the United States for the day, performed by a detail of the Disneyland Security Personnel. The ceremony usually is held between 4 and 5 p.m., depending on the entertainment being offered on Main Street, USA, to prevent conflicts with crowds and music.

Ya: I see. There is also a band in the park, right?

Tom: Yeah, it has been there since the opening of the park, and it plays the role of the Town Band on the Main Street, U.S.A.

Ya: That will be cool. I also want to see the fireworks.

Tom: Yeah, beautiful fireworks are showed at the same time with Disney songs and often appearances from Tinker Bell or Dumbo, flying in the sky above Sleeping Beauty Castle. Scheduling of fireworks shows depends on the time of year. During the slower off-season periods, the fireworks are only offered on weekends. During the busier times, Disney offers additional nights. The park offers fireworks nightly during its busy periods.

Ya: I can imagine.

小丫： 我们在迪士尼乐园能看见或者玩什么？

汤姆： 嗯，有很多东西我们可以玩。他们有很多现场表演的娱乐节目。

小丫： 哦，真的？有什么娱乐节目？

汤姆： 在乐园里可以看到很多童话故事中的人物。他们和游客们打招呼，和孩子们互动，也和人们摆姿势拍照。

小丫： 这么说我可以和米奇、米妮拍照了！

汤姆： 当然可以啊。园里也有很多庆祝活动。

小丫： 什么样的庆祝活动呢？

汤姆： 每天晚上快黄昏时，都有一个军事化的降美国国旗仪式，是由迪士尼乐园的安全部门人员执行的。降旗仪式大概在下午4点到5点之间，取决于当天"中央大街"上的娱乐活动，以免人群和音乐之间有矛盾。

小丫： 我知道了。在乐园里有一支乐队，对吧？

汤姆： 是的，自从建园，乐队就一直在那儿了。他们也扮演着"中央大街"上"小镇乐队"的角色。

小丫： 真酷。我还想看焰火。

汤姆： 没问题。美丽的焰火通常伴随着迪士尼乐园的主题歌曲喷放出来，它们大多以"奇妙仙子"和"小飞象"的形象出现在睡美人城堡的上空。焰火的时间安排取决于当年的时间。在游客偏少的淡季，只有在周末才燃放焰火。在旺季，迪士尼乐园提供额外的焰火之夜，有时整夜都有焰火燃放。

小丫： 我可以想象。

必备词汇

acre
['eikə] n.

土地，地产，英亩

是土地面积的大量单位，一英亩相当于4046.856平方米。 **例如** His garden is about one and a half acre, and he plans to plant vegetables on the land. 他的花园大约有1.5英亩，他想在这块地上种蔬菜。

adjacent
[ə'dʒeisənt] adj.

相邻的，毗连的，接近的

adjacent to 与……相邻，与……相毗邻。类似于next to，但相对正式一些。 **例如** The house adjacent to ours is under repairs. 与我家房子相邻的房子正在修缮。

complex
['kɔmpleks] n.

复合体；综合设施；综合企业，综合结构

一般指众多大楼或一座大楼和诸多辅楼组成的综合建筑群。

例如 They are building a vast new shopping complex in the town. 他们正在市区建造一处大型综合购物楼群。

distinguish
[dis'tiŋgwiʃ] v.

区别，辨别，分别

常用词组有distinguish between...and...在两种事物之间区别，分辨；distinguish from...跟……区分开。 **例如** We can distinguish one kind of flower from another by its color. 我们可以通过颜色把一种花和另一种花区分开来。

entertain
[ˌentə'tein] v.

娱乐，使娱乐；款待

名词形式为entertainment [ˌentə'teinmənt] n. 娱乐，消遣；款待。live entertainment 意为"现场表演的娱乐节目"。

例如 A healthy person should have his family, his work, his entertainment and his friends. 一个健康的人应该有他的家庭、他的工作、他的娱乐和他的朋友。

schedule
['ʃedjuːəl, -dʒuːəl, 'skedʒuːəl,-dʒəl] v.

安排，计划

n. 时间表，计划表，一览表。on schedule 按时，按照预定时间。ahead of schedule 提前。**例如** Let me take a look at the travel schedule for next week. 让我看一下下周的旅行安排。

fan
[fæn] n.

狂热者，粉丝，爱好者，发烧友

例如 Her fans were stormed by her performance and charm. 她的粉丝被她的表演和美丽所倾倒。

initially
[i'niʃəli] adv.

最初，首先，开头

统一的说法有originally, firstly等。
例如 He started initially with reading the alphabet. 他从读字母表开始。

interact
[ˌintə'rækt] v.

相互作用，互动

例如 The singer likes to interact with her fans in the concert. 这位歌手喜欢在演唱会上和粉丝们互动。

conflict [kənˈflikt, ˈkɔnflikt] v.

冲突，抵触；争斗，争执，战斗。n. 冲突，矛盾，斗争

conflict with...冲突，与……抵触。

例如 The teacher is afraid that the hours of those two exams will conflict. 老师担心这两门考试的时间互有冲突。

construction [kənˈstrʌkʃən] n.

建设；建筑物；施工

日常生活中常见的"建筑工地"为 construction site。

例如 The local government raised large sums for highway construction. 地方政府为建设公路筹备了巨额款项。

kid [kid] n.

小孩

这是美国口语中常用的词，一般美国人很少说child。

例如 He often plays with the kids next door. 他经常和邻居家的孩子们一起玩。

parking lot n.

停车场，停车处，多层停车场

例如 If you drive to work, park at the far end of the parking lot. 如果你开车上班，那么把车停在停车场的最远端。

resort [riˈzɔːt] n.

度假村，度假胜地，度假酒店，常去之处

例如 He stayed in a seaside resort for his two-month summer vacation. 他在一座海滨度假村度过了两个月的暑假。

地道美语

1 a military-style flag retreat 一个军事化的降旗仪式。注意短语中military-style的构词形式，用连字符连接两个词变成一个词做定语。类似的说法还有a second-floor apartment 一间在二楼的公寓。例如：

A:　I've always wanted a French-style wedding.

B:　Who doesn't? But you know, it costs a lot of money.

　　A：我一直想要一场法国式的婚礼。

　　B：谁不想呢？但是你要知道，这要花很多钱的。

2 at dusk 傍晚。/ 黄昏时刻。/ 在黄昏。相应地，at dawn 或者at daybreak为在黎明，在破晓时。这样就可以区分at dawn, in the morning, at noon, in the afternoon, at dusk, in the evening 和at night 的区别了。例如：

A:　The birds in my garden start to sing at dawn.

B:　It's a pleasant way to wake up.

　　A：我家花园里的小鸟在破晓时开始歌唱。

　　B：这是个愉快的叫人起床的办法。

3 Impressive. 真叫人印象深刻。/ 真了不起。是对某人惊人技艺的称赞。例如：

A:　You wouldn't believe how well she danced the other night.

B:　I know her dancing is really impressive.

A：你不能相信她那天晚上的舞跳得有多好。

B：我知道她的舞技是多么让人钦佩。

④ Interest is the best teacher. 兴趣是最好的老师。这也是我们汉语中常见的俗语，可见汉语和英语并不是截然不同，也是有很多相似之处的。例如：

A: The girl learned to speak French in two months. It's such a complex language.

B: She's interested in fashion, and Paris is the dream city to her. You know, interest is the best teacher.

A：这个女孩在两个月之内学会了法语。这可是一门很复杂的语言。

B：她对时尚很感兴趣，而且巴黎就是她梦想中的城市。你要知道，兴趣是最好的老师。

⑤ off-season 淡季。相应地，busy season或boom season意为旺季。读者们可不要想当然地以为on-season就是旺季的意思哦。例如：

A: The business of this restaurant is quite good, but the owners take a holiday during the off-season.

B: There's never enough money, so you need to enjoy life when you still have time.

A：这家餐厅的生意很好，但是淡季的时候老板都会休假。

B：钱总是赚不完的，所以你要趁着有时间的时候尽情享受。

6 Dumbo 笨蛋，傻瓜。直译为小飞象，是迪士尼动画《小飞象》中的经典人物，因为剧中小飞象笨手笨脚而被演化为口语中的笨蛋、傻瓜。但并无侵犯之意。

A: How can I do this wrong! I'm such a Dumbo.

B: At least you are as cute as Dumbo. Don't be angry with yourself.

　　A: 我怎么能做错这件事呢！我真是个笨蛋。

　　B: 至少你像小飞象一样可爱。别跟自己生气了。

7 Tinker Bell 奇妙仙子，小叮当。也是迪士尼动画中的经典角色，其中以Tinker Bell（小叮当）最为出名，她为人开朗、热情，为了心中的梦想不懈努力，因此也用来形容拥有这样性格的人。例如：

A: My sister is a Tinker Bell. She's become the most popular student of her school.

B: That's nice. I'm sure all her schoolmates like her.

　　A: 我的妹妹真是个小叮当。她已经变成了全校最受欢迎的学生。

　　B: 这很好啊。我相信她们学校的学生都喜欢她。

表达方式百宝箱

　　本课中我们学习了有关迪士尼乐园的内容，包括它的起源、发展和园内的娱乐项目。大家要注意复习哦。那么现在我们就来总结一下课文中出现的表达方式吧。

Interest is the best teacher. 兴趣是最好的老师。

Not really. 不是很清楚。／不是很喜欢。／不是很想……

There are a whole lot of things that we can do. 那有很多东西我们可以玩。

Many Disney characters can be found throughout the park, greeting visitors, interacting with children, and posing for photos. 在乐园里可以看到很多迪士尼人物，他们和游客打招呼、互动并拍照。

During the busier times, Disney offers additional nights. 在旅游旺季的时候，迪士尼提供额外的焰火之夜。

小丫 带你走遍 美国

迪士尼主题公园——Disneyland Park

迪士尼乐园是一个位于美国加州阿纳海姆市（Anaheim）的主题乐园。由沃特·迪士尼（Walt Disney）一手创办的迪士尼乐园是由沃特迪士尼公司（The Walt Disney Company）所创立与营运的一系列主题乐园与度假区中的第一个，离洛杉矶市中心大约有20分钟的车程（高速公路）。到今天，除了加州洛杉矶迪士尼乐园外，还建造了奥兰多迪士尼乐园、巴黎迪士尼乐园等主题公园。

资格最老的是加州的洛杉矶迪士尼乐园，建成于1955年。1971年，耗时十年的佛罗里达州迪士尼建成；1983年，东京迪士尼建成（2001年，扩建的海上乐园完成，耗资3380亿日元）；1992年，巴黎迪士尼建成，耗资440亿美元。在五大乐园中，位于美国佛罗里达州奥兰多的迪士尼面积最大，有12778公顷，香港迪士尼乐园最小，占地126公顷，仅为佛罗里达州的百分之一。论规模，美国佛罗里达州的奥兰多最大，分为"动物王国"、"魔幻影城"、"科幻天地"和"梦幻世界"四个主题乐园，还有两个水上乐园，全部玩下来至少要五天。

在迪士尼世界中，设有中央大街、小世界、海底两万里、明天的世界、拓荒之地和自由广场等。中央大街上有优雅的老式马车、古色古香的店铺和餐厅茶室等；小世界是专给孩子们设计、为他们所向往的娱乐天地；在"海底两万里"，人们可坐上特制的潜艇，时而来到一片生机勃勃的热带海床，时而又来到阴沉寂寥的寒带海床，尽情观赏五光十色的海底植物和水族，甚至还能看到满载珠宝货物的沉船和因地震陷落海底的古代城市；并可亲自到"月球"上去游览一番；如果来到拓荒之地和自由广场，那就是另一番天地了，在这里人们可以重温当年各国移民在新大陆拓荒的种种情景和英国殖民时期美洲大陆的状况。走在迪斯尼世界中，还经常会碰到一些演员扮成的米老鼠、唐老鸭、白雪公主和七个小矮人，更使人童心复萌、游兴大发。

迪士尼世界不仅是个游乐场，同时又是一个旅游中心，游客来此还可以到附近的海滩游泳、滑冰、驾帆船、到深海捕鱼、乘气球升空，或是参观附近的名胜古迹。这些丰富多彩的节目，给迪士尼世界更增添了几分魅力。

第23课

跳动的音符：参加音乐会

情景介绍: 在西方国家，业余时间人们都会安排很丰富的娱乐活动，比如去野外郊游、和朋友聚会、看电影、听音乐会或者做志愿者。小丫还没有在纽约参加过现场表演的音乐会呢。刚好今天杰西卡邀请小丫一起去听著名的纽约爱乐乐团的音乐会。

会话1

Roommate: Ya, a phone call for you.

Ya: Hello, this is Ya Jiang.

Jessica: Hi, Ya. This is Jessy, tonight there is a splendid concert by the New York Philharmonic. I'd like you to come with me. Are you interested?

Ya: To a concert? I don't know. I prefer staying at home. I was lying on the sofa, and there will be a good film on TV this evening.

Jessica: What? Are you kidding me? Are you telling me that you are staying home for a film? Did I hear it wrong?

Ya: Relax, Jessy. You heard it all right.

Jessica: I can't believe it. That film, you can watch it whenever you want to, but the concert is unique. It's by the New York Philharmonic.

Ya: I've heard about it, but I actually don't know anything about it.

Jessica: Well, let me tell you. It's the oldest symphony orchestra in the States, which was organized in 1842.

Ya: Wow, it's got a long history. I think I should go. I've never been to a concert before.

Jessica: Great! Well, we will go to Avery Fisher Hall this evening, so we need to wear really formal clothes. I'm wearing the fanciest dress I have.

Ya: Let me see. I think I have a dress that I can wear. I wore it once for the wedding party of Tom's cousin. It's a tailored silk dress.

Jessica: That will be perfect. Do I come to your apartment, or we meet in front of Avery Fisher Hall?

Ya: It doesn't matter. Let's meet in front of the music hall.

Jessica: The concert starts at 8:30, so fifteen to eight in front of Avery Fisher Hall? Is it good for you?

Ya: Sure. See you then.

室友： 小丫，你的电话。

小丫： 你好，我是蒋小丫。

杰西卡： 你好，小丫。我是杰西，今天晚上有一场纽约爱乐乐团的音乐会。我想让你跟我一起去。你有兴趣吗？

小丫： 去音乐会？我不知道啊。我还是想待在家。我刚刚就躺在沙发上。今天晚上电视上会播一部很好看的电影。

杰西卡： 你说什么？你在跟我开玩笑吗？你是在说为了一场电影你宁愿待在家里吗？我听错了吗？

小丫： 别紧张，杰西。你没听错。

杰西卡： 我简直不能相信。那场电影你什么时候想看都能看，但是这场音乐会是独一无二的。而且是纽约爱乐乐团。

小丫： 我听说过，但是我还真不太了解。

杰西卡： 我来告诉你。它是美国最古老的交响乐团，创建于1842年。

小丫： 哇，历史这么久远。我想我应该去。我还没参加过音乐会呢。

杰西卡： 太好了！是这样的，我们今天晚上去艾弗里·费雪厅，所以我们要穿很正式的衣服。我要穿我最华丽的裙子。

小丫： 让我想想。我觉得有一条今天可以穿的裙子。我去参加汤姆表哥的婚礼穿的就是这条裙子。是一条定做的丝质连衣裙。

杰西卡： 那就完美了。我是去你的公寓，还是我们在艾弗里·费雪厅前面见面？

小丫：　都可以。我们就在音乐厅前面见面吧。

杰西卡：音乐会8点半开始，我们7点45在艾弗里·费雪厅前面见面？你觉得怎么样？

小丫：　没问题。到时见。

会话2

Jessica: Two tickets for the stalls, please.

Ticketbox: Sorry, it's been sold out. There are only tickets for the balcony. They are cheaper.

Jessica: That's bad.

Ticketbox: You want the first floor or the second floor?

Jessica: Ya, do you have any preference?

Ya: It's all the same to me. It's up to you.

Jessica: All right. Then we'll take two tickets for the first floor.

Ticketbox: Here you are. Two tickets for the first balcony, line 4.

Jessica: How much is it?

Ticketbox: Two tickets…that is 22 dollars, madam.

Jessica: Is there a reduction for students?

Ticketbox: Sure. Can I take a look at your student cards?

Jessica: Here they are.

Ticketbox: Thank you. Then it will be 16 dollars.

杰西卡：　两张正厅的票，谢谢。

售票处：　对不起，正厅的票已经卖完了。现在只有楼座的票。票价更低。

杰西卡： 这可不好。

售票处： 你要一层楼座还是二层楼座？

杰西卡： 小丫，你喜欢一层还是二层？

小丫： 对我来说都一样。你决定吧。

杰西卡： 好吧。那我们要两张一层楼座的票。

售票处： 给你。两张一层楼座的票，第四排。

杰西卡： 多少钱？

售票处： 两张票，那就是22美元，女士。

杰西卡： 学生有优惠吗？

售票处： 当然了。我可以看一下你们的学生证吗？

杰西卡： 给你。

售票处： 谢谢。一共是16美元。

会话3

Jessica: This one is for you, Ya. In the catalogue, you will see what pieces they will play this evening.

Ya: Oh, yes. I need to take a look. I don't know a lot about classical music.

Jessica: I know. We have more different music in the west than in China. This is also the reason I want you to come with me today. I'm curious what you think about it.

Ya: Since 1960s, they have won many honors and awards.

Jessica: Indeed. They have won the award for the best classical album, the best orchestra performance, the best album, for children even, and of course some other awards.

Ya: Thank you for taking me here. What instruments do you have in an orchestra?

Jessica: Well, they have the violin, the viola, the cello, the flute, the clarinet, the harp and many other instruments like...Oh, the concert is going to start. Let's talk about that later.

Ya: Sure.

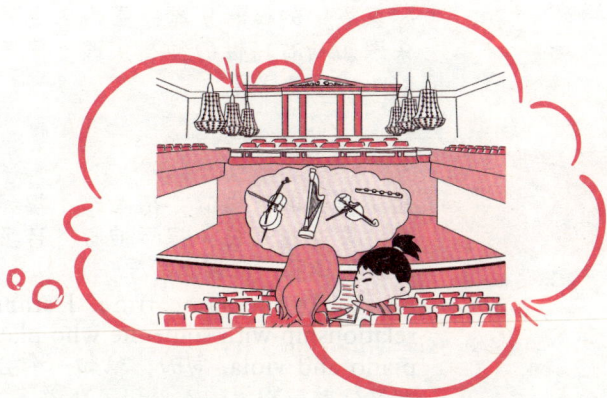

杰西卡： 这个给你，小丫。在目录里你能看见表演的曲目。

小丫： 我得看看，因为我对古典音乐了解不多。

杰西卡： 我知道。中西音乐相差比较大。这也是我今天邀请你来的原因，我很好奇你的反应。

小丫： 70年代的时候，他们就开始获得各种奖项。

杰西卡： 的确如此。他们荣获过"最佳古典音乐专辑奖"、"最佳交响乐团奖"、"最佳儿童专辑奖"和一些别的奖项。

小丫： 真谢谢你请我来。交响乐团都有什么乐器？

杰西卡： 交响乐团主要有小提琴、中提琴、大提琴、长笛、单簧管、竖琴和很多其他乐器。表演马上开始了，我们一会儿再聊。

小丫： 好的。

必备词汇

cello
['tʃeləu] n.

大提琴

这个词需要注意的是读音，不要因为以辅音c开头关就误读为['seləu]。大提琴是提琴家族中的低音乐器、室内主奏的重要乐器和附有特性的独奏乐器，是管弦乐队中的重要成员。

viola
[vi'əulə] n.

中提琴，中提琴演奏者

和小提琴形状相似，稍微比小提琴大一点，拿法指法与小提琴相同，音色不及小提琴华丽，但温润醇厚。

例如 At the same time, I started a relationship with someone who plays the piano and viola. 同时，我和一个会弹钢琴又会拉中提琴的人谈起了恋爱。

concert [kən'sə:t, 'kɔnsə:t] n.

音乐会，演唱会，演奏会

concert hall 音乐厅；go to the concert 去听音乐会，去参加音乐会；solo concert 个人演唱会。**例如** People are queuing up to buy tickets for the concert. 人们正在排队等待买音乐会的入场券。

cousin ['kʌzən] n.

堂兄弟姐妹；表兄弟姐妹

在英语中，没有像汉语中如此之多的表示亲属关系的词语。**例如** I wear this dress to my cousin's wedding last month. 上个月我穿这条裙子去参加了我表妹的婚礼。

clarinet [ˌklæri'net] n.

单簧管，黑管

单簧管也是管弦乐队中的重要乐器之一。**例如** This band only plays the clarinet and the saxophone. 这个乐队只演奏单簧管和萨克斯管。

fancy ['fænsi] adj.

奇特的，昂贵的，精选的

比较级为fancier，最高级为fanciest。**例如** He took his wife to a very fancy restaurant for their anniversary. 在他们的结婚纪念日，他带妻子去了一家很昂贵的餐厅。

harp [hɑ:p] n.

竖琴，四十六弦琴

harp concerto 竖琴协奏曲。**例如** She swept her fingers over the strings of the harp. 她用手指划过竖琴的琴弦。

247

flute
[flu:t] n.

长笛，笛，横笛

注意一个词组champagne flute，意为"香槟杯"，而不是香槟长笛。

例如 During the party, the boy played a very beautiful tune on the flute. 在宴会期间，这位男孩吹奏了一曲非常优美的笛子曲。

Philharmonic
[ˌfilhɑːˈmɔnik, ˌfilə-] n.

交响乐团，爱乐乐团

adj. 交响乐团的，爱好音乐的
Philharmonic orchestra 爱乐乐团，管弦乐团；Berlin Philharmonic 柏林爱乐乐团；New York Philharmonic 纽约爱乐乐团，纽约爱乐交响乐团。

piece
[pi:s] n.

件，杰作

我们熟知的是a piece of paper（一张纸），或者a piece of cake（一块蛋糕），而这里是作为音乐作品的量词。

例如 This is my favorite piece of Mozart. 这是我最喜欢的一首莫扎特的曲子。

balcony
[ˈbælkəni] n.

包厢，戏院楼厅，楼座；阳台

日常生活中常用的意思是"阳台"，然而在音乐厅或歌剧院意思为"楼座，包厢，楼厅"。例如 The tickets for the balcony are sold out. 楼座的票卖光了。

ticketbox n.

售票处

例如 When they were at the ticket box, the young man said to the ticket seller, "Two tickets, please." 来到售票处，小伙子对售票员说："请给我两张票。"

violin
[ˌvaiəˈlin] n.

小提琴，小提琴手

violin concerto 小提琴协奏曲。

例如 The music of the violin blended sweetly with her voice. 小提琴的乐曲和她的嗓音很和谐。

splendid
[ˈsplendid] adj.

辉煌的，灿烂的，极好的，杰出的

例如 The New York Philharmonic is a splendid orchestra. 纽约爱乐乐团是一个杰出的交响乐团。

unique
[juːˈniːk] adj.

独特的，稀罕的，独一无二的

unique opportunity 唯一的机会，难得的机会。**例如** In the eyes of parents, their children are unique and perfect. 在父母眼中，他们的孩子是独一无二的，也是完美的。

stalls
[stɔːlz] n.

正厅前排座位，池座，正厅前座

是在音乐厅或者歌剧院的座位的特殊用语。同义说法有 parterre [pɑːˈtɛə] n. 正厅后座，（剧场的）正厅。

例如 The tickets in the stalls are the most expensive ones. 正厅的座位是最贵的。

地道美语

① Are you kidding me? 你在开玩笑吗？同义句为 Are you joking? 但相比起来，Are you kidding me? 是更为口语化的表达方式。类似的，还可以说 Who are you kidding? 你在跟谁开玩笑？意在指对方自欺欺人。例如：

A: I can speak French without any accent.
B: Who are you kidding? We both know you don't speak French.

　A：我可以不带任何口音地说法语。
　B：你在跟谁开玩笑？我们俩都知道你根本不会说法语。

2 Are you telling me that...? 你是在跟我说……吗？是表示惊讶的说法，类似于汉语中的"不是……吧？"多在熟人或者朋友之间使用。例如：

A: Are you telling me that he's going out with the sister of his ex-girlfriend?
B: True. I saw them yesterday.

　A：你是在告诉我他现在在跟前女友的妹妹约会吗？
　B：没错。我昨天还看见他们了。

3 It doesn't matter. 没关系。我们熟知的回答Sorry 的表达方式，然而在本课中指的是没关系，无所谓的意思。同义的表达方式为It's all the same。

表达方式百宝箱

　本课中我们学习了有关纽约爱乐乐团的简单内容，也学习了如何在音乐厅买票，同时细心的读者会发现，去听音乐会需要穿着正式。现在我们就来复习一下课文中出现过的表达方式吧。

Are you kidding me? 你在跟我开玩笑吗？

Are you telling me that...? 你是在跟我说……吗？

It doesn't matter. 没关系。／无所谓。

It's all the same. 对我来说都一样。／无所谓。

How much is it? 多少钱？

小丫 带你走遍美国

纽约爱乐乐团——New York Philharmonic

纽约爱乐乐团（New York Philharmonic）的正式名称为纽约爱乐交响乐协会（Philharmonic-Symphony Society of New York），是在纽约市于1842年由乌雷利·科雷利·希尔（Ureli Corelli Hill）成立的一支管弦乐团。纽约爱乐是世界上历史最悠久的乐团之一，是美国成立时间最早的乐团，属于美国五大交响乐团之一，并完成了多个音乐作品的美国首演，如贝多芬的《第九交响曲》和柏辽兹的《幻想交响曲》。

1922年，门格尔贝格接任首席指挥后，该团的演奏水平飞速发展。1928年，该团跟纽约交响乐协会合并，形成今天的规模。曾在该团任职的指挥家的名单中，可以看到马勒和达姆罗许等人的名字。从1928年到1936年间，托斯卡尼尼就任音乐监督，该团进入了黄金时代。1958年，当代著名指挥家伯恩斯坦开始指挥该团，使该团进入了第二个黄金时代。乐团在1962年离开卡内基音乐厅搬至艾弗里·费雪厅（林肯中心）之后，人们就一直讨论，乐团回

还是否会更好。从1978年起，印度著名指挥家祖宾·梅塔就任该团的音乐指导与指挥。

　　曾指导过纽约爱乐乐团的大作曲家和大指挥家有：鲁宾斯坦、柴可夫斯基、德沃夏克、魏因加特纳、马勒（任音乐总监）、拉赫玛尼诺夫、理查德·施特劳斯、富特文格勒、托斯卡尼尼（任音乐总监）、斯特拉文斯基、库谢维茨基和沃尔特、伯恩斯坦、祖宾·梅塔等。纽约爱乐乐团闻名于世，与它一些骄人的纪录也是分不开的，德沃夏克的第九交响曲《自新大陆》、拉赫玛尼诺夫的第三钢琴协奏曲由该团首先推出，乐团在美国还首演了贝多芬的第八和第九交响曲、勃拉姆斯第四交响曲、马勒的第一、二、四和第六交响曲、柏辽兹的幻想交响曲等。1986年7月5日，该团在纽约中央公园的一场免费音乐会，吸引了超过80万人，创造了有史以来单场音乐会最高出席人数的纪录。

第24课

感恩节

情景介绍： 感恩节是美国最重要的节日之一，是为了对这一年自己的收获表示感恩。在美国，感恩节是每年11月的第四个星期四。在节日当天，一家人会团聚在一起，享用家庭大餐。为了让小丫感受美国的感恩节，汤姆邀请小丫来他家一起庆祝。

会话1

Tom: Out of bed, sleepyhead. We need to go to get a good spot.

Jerry: What? The sun is not even up yet!

Tom: We are going to the Macy's Thanksgiving Parade! There we can see all the floats and balloons. Sounds exciting, don't you think?

Jerry: Can't we just watch it on TV?

Tom: Nope. This is something you have to see live. Plus I promised to take Ya along.

Jerry: Ok, I'm coming already. Jesus, this is like getting up for Confucius' Birthday Ceremony!

(During the parade)

Jerry: What a prime spot! Look at the big balloons.

Ya: I have never seen such big balloons!

Tom: The parade is about eighty years old. It's a New York tradition.

Ya: Is Santa Claus on that float? Isn't Christmas still one month away?

Jerry: Hah, you are right. Macy is a department store, so they want to get us thinking of Christmas early.

Tom: The idea really works. Some people are proactive. Larry's dad probably already has his Christmas lights up!

Jerry: Or crazy in other words.

汤姆： 起床啦，大懒虫。我们得去占个好位置。

杰瑞： 你说什么呢？太阳还没出来呢！

汤姆： 我们要去看梅西百货的感恩节游行啊。那有好多花车和大气球。听起来多让人激动啊，你不觉得吗？

杰瑞： 我们看电视转播不行吗？

汤姆： 不行。这种东西是一定要现场看的，而且我答应带小丫一起去了。

杰瑞： 好吧，我这就来。天啊，像去参加祭孔大典一样。

（观看游行期间）

杰瑞： 我们的位置太好了。看那些大气球。

小丫： 我从来没见过这么大的气球。

汤姆： 这个游行有大概80年的历史了，是纽约的一项感恩节传统。

小丫： 那个气球上是圣诞老人吗？不是还有一个月才到圣诞节吗？

杰瑞： 哈，你说对了。梅西是家百货公司，所以他们想让我们提前感受圣诞节的气氛。

汤姆： 这个主意真的有效。有些人很有超前意识，像拉里的爸爸，估计他现在已经把圣诞彩灯挂起来了。

杰瑞： 换句话说就是太疯狂。

会话2

Ya: Thank you so much for inviting me. This is my first Thanksgiving. It's the perfect moment to give my thanks to you.

Parents of Tom: You are very welcome, Ya. We enjoy having you here. It's a day of sharing.

Ya: What is the typical dish for Thanksgiving?

Tom: Every year Thanksgiving dinner is one of the biggest family reunions. Turkey and pumpkin pie are the must on the table.

Ya: What's the historic background for Thanksgiving?

Tom: Well, this goes back to the fifteenth century when the first immigrants came over to the United Sates. In the first winter, half of them were suffering from disease and hunger. It was the local Indians who helped them out with their seeds and knowledge. When the new Americans harvested the next year, they held a big celebration in order to show their gratitude towards the Indians. This tradition has been kept ever since. It's a day of family reunion.

Ya: Like our Spring Festival in China?

Tom: Exactly.

Mom of Tom: Hey guys, dinner is ready.

小丫：真感谢你们邀请我。这是我过的第一个感恩节，也是对你们表示感谢的最佳时间。

汤姆的父母：小丫你不用这么客气。我们非常愿意你来。今天是分享的一天。

小丫：感恩节的必备菜肴是什么呢？

汤姆：感恩节是每年最重要的节日之一，这是家庭成员团聚的日子。火鸡和南瓜饼是必备的菜肴之一。

小丫：感恩节的由来是什么呢？

汤姆：这个嘛，要追溯到15世纪第一批移民来到美国的时候。第一年冬天，他们中半数人都死于疾病或饥饿。是当地的印第安人帮助了他们，给他们种子，教他们播种。当第二年新移民收获的时候，他们举办了大型的庆祝活动，来表示对印第安人的感谢。这项传统就这样流传下来。这是家庭团聚的一天。

小丫：就像我们中国的春节。

汤姆：说对了。

汤姆的妈妈：孩子们，晚饭好了。

必备词汇

Macy

美国梅西百货公司

专有名词，因为享誉全球，在使用时不必说Macy Department Store。

例如 The Spiderman balloon floats down central park west during the 86th Macy's Thanksgiving day parade in New York. 在第86届梅西百货感恩节纽约游行中，一个巨大的蜘蛛侠气球飘过中央公园西街。

Confucius
[kənˈfjuʃəs]

孔子；孔子思想

例如 Confucius is the greatest educator in Chinese history. 孔子是中国历史上最伟大的教育家。Confucius schools are started in many western countries. 孔子学院在许多西方国家开展起来。Confucius school 孔子学院。

parade
[pəˈred] n.

游行，（部队的）检阅

例如 A grand Thanksgiving parade is going on in New York.纽约正在举行壮观的感恩节大游行。v. 游行，列队行进。

例如 More than four thousand soldiers, sailors and airmen paraded down the Champs Elysee... 超过4,000名陆、海、空三军将士在香榭丽舍大街游行。

prime
[praim] adj.

最好的，首要的，最初的，基本的
n. 精华，初期，全盛时期

例如 It is one of London's prime locations, near the Big Ben.这是伦敦最好的地段之一，靠近大本钟。We've had a series of athletes trying to come back well past their prime.我们有些早已过了黄金期的运动员仍然想东山再起。

sleepyhead
[ˈslipiˌhɛd] n.

贪睡鬼，瞌睡虫

例如 Since when did you become a sleepyhead? 你从什么时候开始变成一个瞌睡虫了？

proactive
[proˈæktɪv] adj.

积极主动的，先发制人的，主动出击的

reunion
[riˈjunjən] n.

重聚，亲友等聚会；再结合，再统一

例如 The whole family was there for this big family reunion. 全家人都来参加了这次盛大的家庭聚会。

spot
[spɑt] n.

地点，场所；斑点，污点；皮肤上的肿块，斑点

例如 The swimming suit comes in navy with white spots or blue with green spots. 这款游泳衣有藏青色带白色圆点的，也有蓝色带绿色圆点的。

tradition
[trəˈdɪʃən] n.

传统；惯例

例如 Making New Year clothes is their family tradition. 手工制作新年衣服是他们家的传统。traditional adj. 传统的，惯例的。

例如 Spring Festival is one of the most important traditional holidays in China. 春节是中国最重要的传统节日之一。

harvest
['harvist] n.

收割，收获，收成；v. 收获，收割，收到，捕获（动物、鱼等）

例如 Millions of people are threatened with starvation as a result of drought and poor harvests. 几百万人因为干旱和歉收受到饥饿的威胁。在此例句中，drought [draut] n. 干旱，旱季，旱灾。

例如 Spain is suffering one of the worst droughts of the century. 西班牙正遭受着本世纪最严重的旱灾之一。What you harvest is determined by what you sow. 收成的好坏取决于你播下的种子。

地道美语

① Sleepyhead，贪睡鬼，瞌睡虫。是非常口语化的表达方式，对熟悉的人使用。如果是对初认识的人使用，对方可能误认为不尊重。例如：

A: Get up, sleepyhead. I don't have all day waiting for you.

B: I'm getting up. Just one second.

　A: 快起床，贪睡鬼。我可没有一整天的时间等你。

　B: 我这就起来了，再稍等一下。

② We enjoy having you here，我们非常高兴你在这。也可以说 We love having you here。是表示对客人的到来感到高兴甚至荣幸，让客人感到自己是受欢迎的。例如：

A: I hope I don't bother you too much with all these surprise visits.

B: Don't be silly. We love having you here. You are part of our family.

> A: 希望我多次突然到访没有打搅到你们。
>
> B: 别说傻话了。你来我们非常高兴。你就像我们家的一员。

③ **Sounds exciting, don't you think? 听着让人激动，你不觉得吗？反义疑问句征求对方意见，并不期待对方的答案。可以用其他的形容词替换，比如Sounds tiring, don't you think? 听着很累，你不觉得吗？又如，Sounds boring, don't you think? 听着无聊，你不觉得吗？例如：**

A: Anne is going on holiday in Spain, lying on the beach in the sunshine. Sounds relaxing, don't you think?

B: Indeed. I'm jealous of her.

> A: 安妮要去西班牙度假，躺在沙滩上享受阳光。听着就很放松，你不觉得吗？
>
> B: 的确如此，我真羡慕她。

④ **I promised to take Ya along. 我答应带小·丫一起去。这个表达方式中有两处需要注意，一是promise to do something，答应某人做某事；二是take someone along，带某人一起去。例如：**

A: I promised to go home immediately after school, so I can't go to the park with you.

B: We'll call your mom. I don't think she will say no to the park.

A: 我答应过了一放学就回家，所以不能跟你去公园了。

B: 我们可以给你妈妈打电话。我想她不会不让你去公园的。

A: Lucy has never been to the clients on the side of town. Can you take her along when you visit them?

B: No problem. I have a meeting tomorrow. She can come along if she has time.

A: 露西还没去拜访过城那边的客户呢。你去的时候可以带上她吗？

B: 没问题。我明天要去那儿开会。她要是有时间可以一起来。

5 Jesus, this is like getting up for Confucius' Birthday Ceremony! 天啊，像去赶祭孔大典似的！表示好像要去参加非常隆重的仪式，或者去重要的场合。例如：

A: Look, this place is packed with politicians.

B: The annual charity party is as grand as Confucius' Birthday.

A: 看啊，这地方都是政客。

B: 年度慈善晚宴就像祭孔大典一样。

6 Isn't Christmas still one month away? 圣诞节不是还有一个月才到呢吗？值得注意的是away的用法，可以用来表示时间，也可以用来表示距离。例如：

A: When is your next vacation? I know you had a wonderful time in Mexico last year.

B: It's still two months away. This year we are going to Australia.

    A: 你下次什么时候休假？我知道你去年在墨西哥度过了美好的时光。

    B: 还有两个月呢。我们今年去澳大利亚。

A: How far is your fitness center away from your home?

B: It's about 10 kilometers away.

    A: 健身中心离你家多远？

    B: 大概10公里远。

表达方式百宝箱

这节课中出现了一些非常口语化的表达方式，现在我们就来总结一下吧！

I promised to take Ya along. 我答应带小丫一起去。

Isn't Christmas still one month away? 圣诞节不是还有一个月才到呢吗？

Jesus, this is like getting up for Confucius' Birthday Ceremony! 天啊，像去参加祭孔大典似的！

Sleepyhead. 贪睡鬼。

Sounds exciting, don't you think? 听着很让人激动，你不觉得吗？

We enjoy having you here. 你能来我们很高兴。

小丫 带你走遍美国

Thanksgiving Day——感恩节

感恩节（Thanksgiving Day）是由美国人民独创的节日，原意是为了感谢上天赐予的好收成，感谢印第安人的帮助。在美国，自1941年起，感恩节是在每年11月的第四个星期四，像中国的春节一样，在这一天，成千上万的人们不管有多忙，都要和自己的家人团聚。

1620年，一些英国受宗教迫害的清教徒乘坐"五月花"号船去美洲寻求宗教自由。他们在海上颠簸了两个月后，终于在酷寒的11月里，在马萨诸塞州的普利茅斯登陆。在第一个冬天，半数以上的移民都死于饥饿和传染病，危急时刻他们得到了当地印第安人的帮助，活下来的人们在第一个春季即1621年开始播种。整个夏天他们都热切地盼望着丰收的到来，他们深知自己的生存以及殖民地的存在都取决于即将到来的收成。最后，庄稼获得了意外的丰收，为了感谢上帝赐予的丰收，为了感谢印第安人的帮助，他们举行了3天的狂欢活动。从此，这一习俗就此延续下来，并逐渐风行各地。1863年，美国总统林肯宣布每年11月的第四个星期四为感恩节。感恩节庆祝活动便定在这一天，直到现在。届时，家家团聚，举国同庆，其盛大、热烈的情形，不亚于中国人过春节。

在加拿大，感恩节则起始于1879年，是在每年10月第二个星期一，与美国的哥伦布日相同。近年来，感恩节在欧洲甚至中国也渐渐流行起来，大家借此对别人表达谢意。

第25课

帝国大厦

情景介绍: 帝国大厦（Empire State Building），是位于美国纽约市的一栋著名的摩天大楼，共有102层，在很多电影中都曾出现过，更是浪漫爱情故事乐于取景的地点之一。作为电影迷的小丫一直对帝国大厦充满向往，今天就去一睹它的风采吧。

会话1

Ya: I have seen the Empire State Building so many times in movies. Wish I could stand on top of it.

Tom: This wish will easily come true. The only thing you need to do is to get into the elevator.

Ya: You are right. Many things are actually easier than what they seem to be. We just need to get started. Will you join me?

Tom: Sure. Why not? Let's go.

小丫： 我在电影中看过帝国大厦很多次了。真希望我能站到楼顶。

汤姆： 这个愿望太容易实现了。你需要做的唯一一件事就是进电梯。

小丫： 你说得对。许多事情其实比它们看起来的要简单许多。我们只需要开始行动。你要和我一起上去吗？

汤姆： 当然了，为什么不呢？咱们走。

会话2

Ya: Wow, I'm standing on the top of the famous Empire State Building. It's huge. The view is magnificent.

Tom: Exactly. The view is absolutely breathtaking.

Ya: It even makes me a bit dizzy looking down. This is so cool. It's definitely one of the most exciting moments I have experienced in New York.

Tom: Look at me. I need to take a photo for you.

Ya: Along with the Statue of Liberty, the Empire State Building should be the landmark of New York City.

Tom: Liberty and modernity is the characteristic of New York. It's open to everyone with ambition and dreams. There was a time when coming to New York was considered as a daring move. Living here is still the biggest dream of many Americans.

小丫： 哇，我正站在著名的帝国大厦楼顶。真是宏伟的建筑，景色真壮观。

汤姆： 对极了。这景色绝对让人叹为观止。

小丫： 往下看甚至让我有点头晕。太酷了！这绝对是我来纽约以来最让人兴奋的时刻之一。

汤姆： 看我，我得给你拍张照。

小丫： 帝国大厦和自由女神像应该是纽约市的地标。

汤姆： 自由和现代是纽约的城市特点。它向每一个有野心和梦想的人敞开大门。曾经有一段时间，来纽约被认为是很勇敢的行为。直到现在，在纽约定居仍然是很多美国人的梦想。

必备词汇

ambition
[æmˈbɪʃən] n.

抱负，野心；渴望得到的东西；追求的目标；夙愿

例如 His ambition is to sail around the world. 他的梦想就是环球航行。在此句中，ambition与dream通用。又如，Intelligence without ambition is like a bird without wings. 有智慧却没有抱负，就像小鸟没有翅膀。

breathtaking
[ˈbrɛθˌtekɪŋ] adj.

非常激动人心的，惊人的，惊险的，让人喘不过气来的

例如 The hotel has breathtaking views from every room. 这家宾馆的每个房间都有令人惊叹的美景。Some corporations are moving operations out of the US at breathtaking speed. 一些公司正在以惊人的速度搬离美国境内。

magnificent
[mæɡˈnɪfɪsənt] adj.

壮丽的；伟大的；高尚的；华丽的；高贵的

例如 The team played magnificently throughout the competition. 球队在整场比赛中发挥得非常出色。The main railway station is magnificent. 那里最大的火车站宏伟壮观。

intelligence
[ɪnˈtɛlədʒəns] n.

智慧，智力，聪颖

dizzy
[ˈdɪzi] adj.

头昏眼花的；使人眩晕的；引起头晕的

例如 Her head still hurt, and she felt slightly dizzy and disoriented. 她还头疼，并且还晕头转向。disoriented adj. 没有方向感的。

elevator
[ˈɛlə͵vetɚ] n.

电梯，升降机

在英式英语中使用lift。

例如 All skyscrapers are equipped with elevators. 所有的摩天大楼都配有电梯。

landmark
[ˈlænd͵mɑrk] n.

路标；界标；里程碑；纪念碑

例如 The Ambassador Hotel is a Los Angeles landmark. 国宾大饭店是洛杉矶的地标性建筑之一。We supported this landmark legislation. 我们支持这项有里程碑意义的立法。此句中，landmark的意义更为抽象。

modernity
[mɑˈdɚnɪti] n.

现代性

是modern的名词形式。

例如 With incredible energy and determination, she embodies both tradition and modernity. 本着惊人的精力和决心，她很好地将传统与现代结合了起来。

characteristic [ˌkærəktəˈrɪstɪk] n.

特性，特征，特色，性格

例如 This is the characteristic of a young developing country. 这是一个年轻的发展中国家的特征。

liberty [ˈlɪbəti] n.

自由；许可权；解放；释放

例如 This common liberty results from the nature of man. 这种共同自由来自于人的天性。

empire [ˈɛmˌpaɪr] n.

帝国；最高统治权

例如 the Roman Empire 罗马帝国。He is building his publishing empire. 他正在建造他的出版帝国。

Statue of Liberty

自由女神像。专有名词

地道美语

① Many things are actually easier than they seem to be. 许多事情实际上比它们看起来简单。此句型可用于鼓舞听话者。例如：

A: Climbing mountains starts with the first step. Many things are actually easier than they seem to be.

B: Exactly. Most of the time, the first step is the most difficult part.

A: 爬山是由迈出第一步开始的。许多事情实际上比它们看起来简单。

B: 的确是这样。大多数时候，第一步是最困难的。

---

② The view is absolutely breathtaking. 这景色绝对让人叹为观止。breathtaking用于表达景色或其他事物的惊人。例如：

A: He got to where he is now with breathtaking efforts.

B: No success comes easily.

A: 他通过惊人的努力获得了今天的成功。

B: 没有轻而易举的成功。

---

③ The wish will easily come true. 这个愿望可以轻松实现。come true, 梦想或希望实现。

---

④ There was a time when coming to New York was considered as a daring move. 曾有一段时间，来纽约是勇敢的行为。There was a time和once upon a time可以替换。daring意为勇敢，意气用事的。例如：

He was daring and bald when he was young.

他年轻时冲动、鲁莽。

Once upon a time, Antwerp was the biggest port of the world.

曾有一段时间，安特卫普是世界上最大的港口。

表达方式百宝箱

本课中出现了多次表达感慨的句型，现在就让我们一起来总结一下吧。

The wish will easily come true. 这个愿望可以轻松实现。

Many things are actually easier than they seem to be. 许多事情实际上比它们看起来简单。

The view is absolutely breathtaking. 这景色绝对让人叹为观止。

小丫带你走遍美国

帝国大厦——Empire State Building

帝国大厦（Empire State Building），是位于美国纽约市的一栋著名的摩天大楼，共有102层，由Shreeve, Lamb, 和Harmon建筑公司设计，1930年动工，1931年落成，只用了410天，它的名字来源于纽约州的别称帝国州（Empire State），所以英文原意实际上是"纽约州大厦"，而"帝国州大厦"是以英文字面意思直接翻译的译法，但帝国大厦的译法已广泛流传，而且似乎给这座地标性建筑增添了一份霸气，故沿用至今。

帝国大厦位于曼哈顿第五大道350号，夹在34大街与33大街之间，是纽约市著名的旅游景点之一。它的顶部的泛光灯的颜色会因时间或重大事件而改变，比如说在911事件后就亮了3个月的蓝色灯，以示哀悼。建筑历史学家威里斯说，今天的帝国大厦一方面象征美国工商业文化，另一方面也是纽约甚至是全美国的永远地标。

帝国大厦的顶层一直是文艺界喜爱取景的地方，自大厦建成后，共有90多部电影选择这里作为取景点，其中包括《金刚》和《西雅图不眠夜》等经典电影。帝国大厦既是一座多功能的写字楼，同时也是纽约市最著名的旅游景点之一，成千上万的游客每天在这里排队等候电梯登顶观景。自1994年以来，帝国大厦已成为青年人到顶层举行婚礼和纽约人庆祝情人节的传统场所。在这里举行过婚礼的人，就能成为帝国大厦俱乐部的成员，每年情人节都可以免费重返帝国大厦。不过，要取得在大厦举行婚礼的资格并不容易，新人要写信给帝国大厦，描述他们为什么要在大厦举行婚礼，之后大厦根据申请人的情况和是否有原创性等条件，挑选出最佳人选。

可见，小丫此次的帝国大厦之行是非常有纪念意义的。

第26课

美式大餐：自己做饭乐趣多

情景介绍：一提到美国饮食，人们首先想到的是麦当劳、肯德基等快餐，或者汉堡包、炸薯条和碳酸饮料。其实，美国大餐不仅局限于这些，还包括牛排、沙拉、甜点、各式汤类等等。大学生包括留学生自己做饭是经常的事，既美味又简单的菜肴有哪些呢？小丫要以身试菜，带我们领略美国大餐的风采。

会话1

Tom: What are you doing in the kitchen?

Jerry: I'm thinking of cooking dinner tonight. Any ideas or suggestions about what I should make?

Tom: What about roast chicken? Or hamburger?

Jerry: I will go for roast chicken.

Tom: All right. Let's see what we need for roast chicken.

Jerry: I'm making a shopping list right now. What vegetables would you like?

Tom: What about some herbs and potatoes?

Jerry: What herbs?

Tom: Dill and rosemary goes well with chicken.

Jerry: No problem, I'm putting them down on the list. What about dessert?

Tom: Why don't we take ice cream for dessert?

Jerry: Ice cream sounds great! What about chocolate and vanilla flavored?

Tom: Sounds perfect to me.

Jerry: I don't have much cash left with me. I need to stop by the ATM before going to the supermarket, which might take a while.

Tom: Take your time. We are not in a rush.

汤姆：	你在厨房干什么呢？
杰瑞：	我打算做晚饭。有什么想法或建议吗？
汤姆：	烤鸡怎么样？或者汉堡？
杰瑞：	我想吃烤鸡。
汤姆：	好的。我们需要买些什么菜吗？
杰瑞：	我正在列一个购物清单。你想吃什么蔬菜？
汤姆：	买一些香料和土豆怎么样？
杰瑞：	什么香料？
汤姆：	小茴香和迷迭香跟鸡肉一起做很不错。

杰瑞: 没问题，我把它们写在购物清单上。甜点吃什么呢？

汤姆: 冰淇淋怎么样？

杰瑞: 冰淇淋好极了！我们买巧克力和香草口味的如何？

汤姆: 我觉得好极了。

杰瑞: 我身上没什么现金。去超市之前我得先去提款机取点钱，所以可能需要一点时间。

汤姆: 慢慢来，我们不着急。

会话2

Ya: I'd like to help pitch in with dinner.

Tom: Really? You're joking.

Ya: No. I'd like to do something special for you on your birthday.

Tom: I'd like that. Alright, put on this apron first.

Ya: OK. Now how can I help?

Tom: Hmm, let me see. Boil some water and then whisk two eggs.

Ya: Easy. I could do that with my eyes closed. (After a while) Done.

Tom: Not bad. Okay, now take some meat and potatoes from the fridge.

Ya: How many potatoes do you need?

Tom: Three. And bring four bell peppers.

Ya: Gotcha. OK. Here they are.

Tom: Now wash them, then dice the potatoes and bell peppers. Then slice the meat.

Ya: Where's the peeler?

Tom: It's in the cabinet.

Ya: Oh, I cut my finger.

Tom: Let me take a look at that. I can't stop the bleeding. We need to go to the hospital.

Ya: I guess cooking is not as easy as I thought.

小丫:	我想帮忙准备晚饭。
汤姆:	真的吗？你开玩笑的吧。
小丫:	不是，我想在你生日那天做点特别的菜。
汤姆:	我喜欢这个主意。好吧，先把围裙穿上。
小丫:	好的，现在我能做点什么呢？
汤姆:	让我想想，先烧水，然后打两个鸡蛋。
小丫:	简单，我闭着眼睛都能做。（一段时间后）好了！
汤姆:	不错嘛。现在从冰箱里拿出一些肉和土豆。
小丫:	你要几个土豆？
汤姆:	三个。再拿四个青椒。
小丫:	明白了，没问题。先给你土豆。
汤姆:	现在洗土豆，把土豆和青椒切成块儿，然后把肉切成丝。
小丫:	削皮刀在哪儿？

汤姆：　在柜子里。

小丫：　啊呀，我切到手了。

汤姆：　让我看看。我止不住血。我们得去医院。

小丫：　看来做饭不像我想的那么简单。

必备词汇

apron
['eprən] n.

围裙

例如 An apron prevents you from making your clothes dirty while cooking. 围裙可以防止你在做饭时把衣服弄脏。

dice
[daɪs] v.

将……切成小方块

例如 Dice the onion. 把洋葱切成小块。

dill
[dɪl] n.

小茴香，草茴香。一种做菜用的香料

flavored

flavor的过去式和过去分词，给……调味，给……增加风味

例如 Some flavored waters are made with water and real juice. 一些有味道的饮料是用水和真正的果汁混合成的。

hamburger
['hæm,bɜ·gə·] n.

汉堡包

herb
[hɜ·b] n.

草，草本植物；药草；香草

Many herbs are used to add flavors in the kitchen.许多香草在厨房中使用，以增添食物的味道。

peeler
['pilə·] n.

去皮器，削皮器

是peel的名词形式。例如 a potato peeler 土豆削皮器。Can you please peel the potato? 你能削土豆皮吗？

pitch in
(with sth)

加入进来帮忙（做某事）

例如 If we all pitch in, we'll have it finished in no time. 如果我们大家都加入进来帮忙做，我们马上就能完成了。

roast
[rost] v.

烤，烘

例如 Roasted turkey is a traditional dish for Thanksgiving. 烤火鸡是传统的感恩节菜肴。

rosemary
['roz,mɛri] n.

迷迭香

| shopping list | 购物清单 |

slice
[slaɪs] v.

切成片
例如 Helen sliced the cake. 海伦把蛋糕切成了片。

vanilla
[vəˈnɪlə] n./ adj.

香草味的，香草的

whisk
[wɪsk] v.

搅拌；挥动
例如 Just before serving, whisk the cream. 在使用之前，要先搅拌一下奶油。

地道美语

① Any ideas or suggestions about what I should make? 有什么想法或者建议吗？简单用法是Any ideas? 用于征求对方意见。例如：

A: I'm doubting between Spain and France for my vacation? Any ideas?

B: I prefer Spain. Barcelona is my favorite city.

A: 我对去西班牙还是法国度假犹豫不决，有什么建议吗？

B: 我更喜欢西班牙。巴塞罗那是我最喜欢的城市。

---

② **Gotcha. 没问题。／抓住你了。／听懂了。是非常口语化的表达方式。例如：**

A: In this case, you need to take the real schedule into account.

B: Gotcha.

　A: 在这种情况下，你要考虑到实际的计划。

　B: 没问题，我明白了。

---

③ **I could do that with my eyes closed. 我闭着眼睛都能做。表示所要做的事情异常简单。例如：**

A: Can you put the glasses in the cabinet?

B: Sure. I can do that with my eyes closed.

　A: 你能把杯子放回到柜子里去吗？

　B: 当然了。我闭着眼睛都能做。

---

④ **I will go for roast chicken. 我想吃烤鸡。go for是表示选择的表达方式。例如：**

A: Which dress do you think looks better, the red one or the blue one?

B: If I were you, I would go for the red one.

　A: 哪条裙子更好看？红色的还是蓝色的？

　B: 如果我是你，我就选红色的。

---

⑤ **Really? You're joking. 真的吗？你开玩笑的吧。表示不相信对方的话。例如：**

A: I'm going to learn diving this summer.
B: Really? You're joking. We don't live on the coast.

A: 这个夏天我要学潜水。
B: 真的吗？你开玩笑的吧。我们不住在海边。

6 Take your time. We are not in a rush. 慢慢来，我们不着急。例如：

A: Can you wait a second? I still need to pack my bag.
B: Take your time. We still have 3 hours before the plane takes off.

A: 你能等我一会儿吗？我还得收拾行李。
B: 不着急，离飞机起飞还有三个小时呢。

表达方式百宝箱

　　在本课中出现了有关做饭、征求意见等多方面的表达方式，现在就让我们一起总结一下吧。

Any ideas or suggestions about what I should make? 有什么想法或建议吗？

I could do that with my eyes closed. 我闭着眼睛都能做。

I don't have much cash left with me. 我身上没有多少现金。

I will go for roast chicken. 我想吃烤鸡。

Really? You're joking. 真的吗？你开玩笑的吧。

Stop by. 路过。

Take your time. We are not in a rush. 慢慢来，我们不着急。

Why don't we take ice cream for dessert? 我们甜点吃冰淇淋怎么样？

小丫 带你走遍 美国

美国冰淇淋——哈根达斯 （Haagen-Dazs）

冰淇淋是深受年轻人喜欢的甜品。美国著名冰淇淋品牌哈根达斯在中国享有盛誉，更重要的是其价格不菲。哈根达斯（Haagen-Dazs）作为美国冰淇淋品牌，1921年由鲁本·马特斯(Reuben Mattus)研制成功，并于1961在美国纽约布朗克斯命名并上市。它亦成立了连锁雪糕专门店，在世界各国销售其品牌雪糕，在54个国家或地区共开设超过700间分店。

哈根达斯主要口味有香草、巧克力、草莓、抹茶、曲奇香奶、牛奶太妃、夏威夷果仁、芒果、咖啡、葡萄兰姆酒、提拉米苏等。甜品包括了浪漫奇缘分、浓情蜜意、宠爱一生、给我的爱、心醉浪漫、爱琴海之舟梦、伊甸园等等。

哈根达斯冰淇淋，1921年诞生于纽约布朗克斯市的一个家庭。哈根达斯是冰淇淋品牌的一个神话，它的诞生套用一句时下流行的话来说，就是纯属偶然。哈根达斯之父是一个叫鲁本.马特斯的波兰人，靠销售水果冰起家，积累了自己的第一桶金。在其他冰品制造商以降低产品价格进行竞争时，例如在冰品中加入安定剂、防腐剂及增加空气含量的同时，马塔斯决心制造最好的冰淇淋，而坚持使用纯净、最天然的原料。马塔斯为他的冰淇淋取了一个丹麦名字——Haagen-Dazs，他认为这个斯堪的纳维亚的名字可以唤起人们对新鲜、天然、健康及高品质的追求。而最早的哈根达斯冰淇淋只有香草、巧克力和咖啡三种口味，草莓是第四种。现今，哈根达斯已经被视为冰淇淋品牌中的贵族。如今，不仅在全美，在全球都是极受欢迎的品牌。无论在哪里，一提到"哈根达斯"，人们就会想起极其美味诱人的冰淇淋，在中国也是如此，它似乎更像是优质生活和品味的象征。

感受时尚：纽约时装周

情景介绍：纽约时装周（New York Fashion Week）与巴黎、米兰、伦敦时装周并称全球四大时装周，每年举办两次，2月份举办当年秋冬时装周，9月份举办次年的春夏时装周。在纽约可谓是近水楼台，喜欢时尚的小丫绝对不能错过这样的机会。

The first New York Fashion Week (which was then called "Press Week") was the world's first ever organized fashion week. First held in 1943, the event was designed to attract attention away from the French fashion during World War II, when fashion industry insiders were unable to travel to Paris to see French fashion shows. Fashion publicist Eleanor Lambert organized an event which she called "Press Week" to showcase American designers for fashion journalists, who had previously neglected their innovations. (Buyers were not admitted to the shows, and instead had to visit designers' showrooms.) Press Week was a success, and fashion magazines like Vogue, which were normally filled with French designs, increasingly featured American fashion.

Since 2009, Mercedes-Benz officially became the sponsor of the event, and New York Fashion Week was called "Mercedes-Benz Fashion Week" from then.

第一届纽约时装周（当时称为"出版周"）是世界上首次有组织的时装周。首次举办于1943年，目的在于将人们对二战中集中在法国时尚的注意力吸引回来。因为当时的战争，时装界的内部人士无法到法国去观看时装秀。时尚杂志编辑埃莉诺·兰伯特组织了一场被她称为是"出版周"的秀来向时尚记者们介绍美国的设计师。在此之前，美国的本土设计经常受到时尚出版界的忽视。（消费者不允许入场，相反只能去设计师的展览室）。"出版周"很成功，像《时尚》这类通常充满法国设计的时尚杂志开始大量展现美国时尚。

从2009年开始，梅赛德斯-奔驰成为了纽约时装周的赞助商，因此纽约时装周也从此称为"梅赛德斯时装周"。

必备词汇

attract
[ə'trækt] vt.

吸引；诱惑；引起……的好感（兴趣）
常用搭配为attract one's attention，译为吸引某人的注意力。例如 The Cardiff Bay is attracting many visitors. 加的夫海湾项目吸引了众多游客。

design
[dɪˈzaɪn] n./ v.

设计，计划

designer，设计师。过去式和过去分词为designed。**例如** These boots are specially designed for men. 这些靴子是专门为男士设计的。

innovation
[ˌɪnəˈveɪʃən] n.

改革，创新，新观念

例如 We must promote originality and encourage innovation. 我们必须提倡创意，鼓励革新。

neglect
[nɪˈɡlɛkt] v.

疏忽；忽略；遗漏

例如 The woman denied that she had neglected her child. 那位妈妈不承认她对自己的孩子不管不问。

sponsor
[ˈspɑnsə] n.

发起者，主办者，担保者，赞助者

例如 Many airports sponsor classes run by therapists or pilots. 许多机场都会赞助由治疗师或飞行员开设的课程。

press
[prɛs] n.

新闻报道；出版物；印刷厂

例如 Who leaked the news to the press? 是谁把消息泄露给新闻界的？

previously
[ˈpriːvɪəslɪ] adv.

事先，以前

例如 Previously she had very little time to work in her own garden. 以前，她没什么时间打理自己的花园。

showcase ['ʃoˌkes] vt.

使展现，在玻璃橱柜陈列

例如 Restored films are being showcased this month at a festival in Paris. 本月的巴黎电影节将展映一些修复版的电影。

feature ['fitʃɚ] n.

特征，特点；v. 描写……的特征

例如 This spectacular event, now in its 5th year, features a stunning catwalk show. 这一盛事如今已是第5个年头，其重头戏是一场精彩纷呈的时装秀。

地道美语

下面介绍一些有关时尚的地道美语表达方式：

1 cat show 时装秀，T台秀。人们所说的猫步就来源于此。例如：

Fashion festivals are always featured by cat shows.

时装节总是以T台秀为特点。

2 dressed to kill 迷死人的打扮。意思当然不是穿上蒙面的紧身衣去干杀人的勾当，而是用来表示dressed extremely well, wearing fashionable clothing。穿着出众，打扮时尚，漂亮的打扮迷死众生，让人甘拜在你的石榴裙下。例如：

Tina was dressed to kill for her date on Saturday night.

周六的晚上，蒂娜打扮得漂漂亮亮地去赴约了。

It took Mary two hours to get ready, but it was worth it–she was dressed to kill and became the center of attention. Everyone was saying she was the most beautiful woman at the prom.

> 玛丽为参加毕业舞会花了两个钟头打扮。然而工夫不负有心人，她穿戴得美丽动人，成为受人瞩目的焦点。谁都说她是毕业舞会上最漂亮的小姐。

③ fashion victim 时尚的牺牲品，一味地赶时髦而穿着不得体。意大利时尚品牌Versace的创始人说，"When a woman alters her look too much from season to season, she becomes a fashion victim." 也就是说，当一个女人随着季节的变化改变自己的容貌时，她已经成为时尚的牺牲品。例如：

A: Look at Lucy. Doesn't she look ridiculous in that dress? It doesn't suit her at all.

B: Yeah she's only wearing it because she saw it in a magazine. She's such a fashion victim.

> A: 看看露西，她穿那条裙子看起来荒谬极了，根本不搭。
>
> B: 是啊，她穿这条裙子就因为在时尚杂志里看见过。她就是一个时尚的牺牲品。

④ Wardrobe malfunction 走光。在娱乐新闻中常见的走光一词，正确表达方法即为wardrobe malfunction。例如：

Wardrobe malfunction has been used by some people to catch attention of the Media.

> 走光已经成为一些人用来吸引媒体注意的方法。

小丫 带你走遍美国

纽约时装周——New York Fashion Show

1943年，由于受第二次世界大战影响，时装业内人士无法到巴黎观看法国时装秀，因而纽约时装周在美国应运而生。它也因此成为世界上历史最悠久的时装周。1993年，纽约时装周开始在纽约曼哈顿的布赖恩特公园举办，T台被安置在一个个白色帐篷内，只有受邀的买家、业内人士、媒体和各界名人方能入场。

据美国时装设计师协会统计，从10日到17日的8天里，纽约市将有大大小小、各种形式的时装走秀750余场。该协会主席史蒂文·科尔布告诉记者："对于年轻而富有创新精神的设计师来说，这次时装盛宴是一个不容错过的大好机会。"受经济下滑影响，设计师们还需要花些心思考虑如何让买家主动"掏腰包"，独特的配饰成为他们的好帮手。在著名设计师马克·雅各布的秀场上出现了缀满小珍珠的发饰，新颖别致；腰带的出镜率也很高，从材料到宽度都各有不同，甚至也成为晚礼服和高腰泳衣上不可或缺的装饰。2009年9月，美宝莲纽约首次作为赞助商为纽约时装周派出一支才华横溢的彩妆师团队，由全球彩妆大师Charlotte Willer领衔。Willer深受全球广告和平面摄影师的喜爱，她对色彩和创新的热爱与激情赢得了全球时尚界的尊重。

纽约时装周每年举办两次，2月举办当年秋冬时装周，9月举办次年春夏时装周。纽约时装周每年吸引观众逾23万人次，为纽约创收16亿美元。

第28课

纽约的秋天

情景介绍: 纽约是个四季分明的地方。秋天来临时, 树叶渐渐变成金黄色, 随风飘落在路上、停在路边的车上, 甚至行人的肩头, 想象这画面是何等浪漫。

会话1

Ya: The weather in New York is beautiful.

Tom: Fall is the best season in New York, you know.

Ya: Yes, I can see. The summer heat is over, and the winter cold is still far away.

Tom: What is the weather like in Beijing at this time of this year?

Ya: Autumn is also very nice in Beijing. Leaves have different colors and are falling off trees.

Tom: Is it very cold in winter?

Ya: No, it isn't, but sometimes it snows in winter, and it can be very windy.

Tom: Does it rain a lot in summer in Beijing?

Ya: Oh, yes, sometimes it rains heavily. How about here in New York?

Tom: We also have a lot of rain here but it hardly rains in fall.

Ya: Right. I felt it's rather dry here.

Tom: It's true. Many people from the south don't like the weather here.

小丫: 纽约的天气真美。

汤姆: 你知道吗，秋天是纽约最美的季节。

小丫: 是啊，我看得出来。夏天的热浪已经过去，寒冷的冬天还没到来。

汤姆: 北京这个时候的天气怎么样？

小丫: 北京的秋天也很美。树叶变成不同的颜色，从树上掉下来。

汤姆: 北京的冬天冷吗？

小丫: 不太冷，但是有时下雪，并且风很大。

汤姆: 北京夏天经常下雨吗？

小丫: 是啊，有时还下得很大。纽约怎么样？

汤姆: 纽约也下雨，但是秋天基本不下。

小丫: 是啊，我觉得这里的气候比较干燥。

汤姆: 真是这样。许多南方人不喜欢纽约的天气。

会话2

Ya: Tom, what is your favourite season?

Tom: Summer is my favourite season, because I can go swimming in the river, and it's so relaxing and refreshing.

Ya: I don't like summer at all.

Tom: Why not?

Ya: Because it's very hot. What's more, the strong sunlight is damaging to our skin.

Tom: That's true, but you can always put on sun cream. What about you? What's your favourite season?

Ya: I like fall the best. The weather is cooling down. Plus fall is the season for harvest. It's the moment to enjoy what you have created.

Tom: I see why you like fall.

小丫： 汤姆，你最喜欢哪个季节？

汤姆： 夏天是我最喜欢的季节，因为我可以去河里游泳，很放松，又让人充满活力。

小丫： 我一点也不喜欢夏天。

汤姆： 为什么呢？

小丫： 因为夏天太热，而且强烈的阳光伤害我们的皮肤。

汤姆： 是这样，但是你可以用防晒霜。你呢，你最喜欢的季节是什么？

小丫： 我最喜欢秋天。天气逐渐转凉，而且秋天是收获的季节。是个享受一年劳动成果的时刻。

汤姆： 我明白你为什么喜欢秋天了。

必备词汇

fall [fɔl] n.

秋季，秋天；adj. 秋季的，秋天的

美式英语习惯用fall而不是autumn来表达秋天。**例如** Likewise for journalists blocking out a fall travel schedule. 这就如同记者确定秋季的行程安排一样。

hardly ['hɑrdli] adv.

几乎不；简直不；刚刚

例如 I hardly know the man living next door. 我几乎不认识住在隔壁的男子。

heat [hit] n.

热，热度，高温；热烈，激烈

例如 Some people can't cope with the heat and humidity. 一些人无法忍受高温和潮湿。

英语征服记

sun cream
[sʌn krim] n.

防晒霜

例如 She puts her toddler out in the sun with no sun cream for 10 to 15 minutes every day. 她每天把孩子暴露在阳光下10到15分钟，而且不涂防晒霜。

windy
['wɪndi] adj.

有风的

例如 New York is known for its harsh windy winters. 纽约广为人知的就是它严酷的冬天。

地道美语

1. If Winter comes, can Spring be far behind? 冬天来了，春天还会远吗？出自雪莱的诗句，预示新的希望即将到来。例如：

A: I don't know what is going to happen with my job? The company is firing a lot of people.

B: Don't be so negative. If Winter comes, can Spring be far behind?

　　A: 不知道我的工作会怎么样。我们公司在大裁员。

　　B: 别这么消极。如果冬天来了，春天还会远吗？

2 what's more. 另外。类似的表达方式还有more over, further more。例如：

The United States has a large territory, more over, it has the strongest economy of the world.
美国有辽阔的领土，而且有世界上最发达的经济。

表达方式百宝箱

在英语中与雨有关的谚语有很多，下面就让我们一起来看看吧。

Red sky at night, sailor's delight. Red sky in the morning, sailor takes waring. 早霞不出门，晚霞行千里。

If bees stay at home, rain will soon come. If they fly away, fine will be the day. 蜜蜂迟归，雨来风吹。

Halo around the sun or moon, rain or snow soon. 日晕三更雨，月晕午时风。

小丫带你走遍美国

飓风

飓风指大西洋和北太平洋东部地区形成的强大而深厚的热带气旋，其意义和台风类似，只是产生地点不同。飓风一词源自加勒比海言语的恶魔Hurican，亦有说是玛雅人神话中创世众神的其中一位，就是雷暴与旋风之神Hurakan。而台风一词则源自希腊神话中大地之母盖亚之子Typhon，它是一只长有100个龙头的魔物，传说其孩子就是可怕的大风。至于中文"台风"一词，有人说源于日语，亦有人说来自中国广东话"大风"的发音，传至国外后再次传回国内译为台风。以前，中国东南沿海经常有风暴，当地渔民统称其为"大风"，后来变成台风。

美国几乎每年都要遭受不同程度的飓风的袭击。1900年9月袭击德克萨斯州加尔维斯敦的飓风是美国历史上造成死亡人数最多的一次飓风。造成的死亡人数估计在8000人至12000人之间。飓风引发了洪水，淹没了加尔维斯敦城的12个街区。

第29课

听广播

情景介绍： 类似于我国音乐之声、交通广播等，美国也有众多针对不同听众的电台。在开车或者休息之余，听听广播是获得各种信息的重要途径。另外，众所周知，听英文广播绝对是提高听力乃至整体英语水平的好办法，因此小丫也经常收听广播，既听新闻又练英语，真是一举两得。

短文1

The winter weather will stay. There is still no end for the coldness. Later tonight the temperature along the coast will become -10 to -2 Celsius Degree. Tomorrow we are expecting a slight increase of the temperature. The following night will witness another freezing, but no snow is coming.

冬季天气仍将延续。寒冷的天气还没有结束。今天夜间海边气温将达到零下10到零下2摄氏度。明天气温将稍微有所回升。明天夜间气温将再次达到零下，但是不会下雪。

短文2

On E40 in Washington, a heavy accident happened around 3 o'clock this afternoon. 4 people died, and 3 were badly injured. In the direction to D.C. the traffic has to become one lane.

在华盛顿的E40上，今天下午三点左右发生了一起严重的交通事故。4人死亡，3人严重受伤。去D.C.方向的车辆必须汇成一列。

短文3

In the second half of last year, the total number of unemployed people in the States has again dropped. At this moment, there are still 200, 000 people unemployed, which is about 3% of the active population. In southern states, the unemployment rate is slightly higher, where more than 35% of the young people don't have a job.

去年下半年，美国的失业率再创新低。在截稿时，仍然有大约20万人没有工作，这大概占有劳动力人口总数的3%。在南方各州，失业率稍高，大概有35%以上的年轻人没有工作。

必备词汇

coast
[kost] n.

海岸，海边

例如 Camp sites are usually situated along the coast, close to beaches. 野营地一般都位于海滨，靠近沙滩。

injure
['ɪndʒɚ] vt.

损害，毁坏；（尤指事故中）伤害

例如 A number of bombs have exploded, seriously injuring at least five people. 数个炸弹爆炸，造成至少5人重伤。

lane
[len] n.

小路，小巷；规定的单向行车道，车道

例如 The lorry was travelling at 20mph in the slow lane. 卡车在慢车道上以20英里的时速行驶。

slight
[slaɪt] adj.

微小的，细小的

例如 Doctors say he has made a slight improvement. 医生说他的病情稍有好转。

unemployed
[ˌʌnɛmˈplɔɪd] adj.

被解雇的，失业的，不在使用中的，未用的

例如 Have you been unemployed for over six months? 你失业有6个多月了？

witness
['wɪtnɪs] v.

做记录；提供或作为……的证据；见证

例如 I'd rather address the tomb as a historic witness than a nameless destination. 我宁愿以一座坟墓当作历史的见证人而非默默无闻地死去。

地道美语

① 4 people died, and 3 were badly injured. 4人受伤，3人死亡。

广播的特点是语言简要，用有限的词汇表达尽可能丰富的意义。例如：

In the flood yesterday, two children were reported missing.

在昨天的洪水中，有两名儿童被报失踪。

② The total number of unemployed people in the States has again dropped. 美国的总失业人数再创新低。例如：

The interest rate of saving in the bank has again touched the bottom.

银行存款利率再次触底。

③ The winter weather will stay. 冬季的寒冷天气仍将持续。例如：

A: We are suffering from a long winter this year. The temperature doesn't seem to go up.

B: The winter weather will stay till May. It's indeed a very long winter.

A: 今年的冬天特别长。气温没有回升的迹象。

B: 冬季的天气要持续到五月份。的确是个很长的冬天。

---

4 Tomorrow we are expecting a slight increase of the temperature。明天气温将稍有回升。expect在这里指我们基本确定要发生的事。例如：

Due to the strike of public transport, we are expecting a big traffic jam on the highway.

由于公共交通罢工，高速公路上的交通堵塞将会很严重。

表达方式百宝箱

4 people died, and 3 were badly injured. 4人死亡，3人受重伤。

The total number of unemployed people in the States has again dropped. 美国的总失业人数再创新低。

The winter weather will stay. 冬季的寒冷天气仍将持续。

Tomorrow we are expecting a slight increase of the temperature. 明天气温将稍有回升。

小丫 带你走遍美国

美国有线电视新闻网（Cable News Network）——CNN

　　CNN是美国有线电视新闻网（Cable News Network）的英文缩写，由特纳广播公司（TBS）董事长特德·特纳于1980年6月创办，通过卫星向有线电视网和卫星电视用户提供全天候的新闻节目，总部设在美国佐治亚州的亚特兰大。

　　任何突发的新闻，CNN国际新闻网都会率先为您做现场报道。全球超过210个国家及地区均转播CNN的新闻。凭借先进的技术，第一时间现场为您详尽地报道全球新闻的始末，令您仿佛置身其中。

　　CNN国际新闻网除了将全球新闻送到府上外，还加强了对亚洲地区新闻的报道。亚洲七个新闻分社设在香港、东京、北京、首尔、雅加达、新德里及曼谷，将有关整个亚洲时事的头条新闻、专题节目及报道，精确地传送到世界各地。此外，CNN国际新闻网还通过设于香港的制作中心，制作集中探讨亚洲地区问题的节目，借此为观众报导有关亚太区主要的社会、文化及商业发展的动态。《亚洲世界新闻》（World News Asia）报道亚洲区及世界各地的新闻。每逢周末播出的半小时《亚洲透视》（Inside Asia）集中地探讨亚洲时事及社会问题，而《亚洲新闻》（Asia This Day）则是一个由香港播出的全新半小时清晨新闻节目。

　　其他的专题节目也可以为您带来有关生活和时尚的新闻，《流行登陆》（Style with Elsa Klensch）披露时装设计行业的专业意见。《赖利金现场》（Larry King Live）云集世界领袖、新闻人物及各地名人于府上，与您谈天说地。《世界体坛》（World Sports）报道的体育快讯，令您每天都紧跟国际体坛的动态及盛事。《好莱坞万花筒》（Showbiz Today）、《电脑新世界》（Travel Guide）等节目则专门向您提供这些地区内最新的趋势及消息。

第30课

去药店买药

情景介绍： 在美国，药店卖药和去药店买药的管理都很严格，处方药必须在医生的指导下才能购买。一些在国内视为非处方药的药品，在美国也是处方药。买药时要出示医生的开药证明。大小药店都有专业的药剂师供顾客咨询。

会话1

(Ya in the pharmacy.)

Pharmacist: Who is next?

Ya: Me. I think it's my turn now.

Pharmacist: Do you have a prescription, Miss?

Ya: Yes, here you are.

Pharmacist: All right. These are pills. It's antibiotics. You take them three times a day, two pills each time. Remember to take them before meals, otherwise it might cause problem in your stomach. You can't drink alcohol with the pills. This is syrup. You drink one teaspoonful from the bottle twice a day till your coughing gets better.

Ya: Will the syrup be sufficient? I've really been coughing a lot.

Pharmacist: Normally it should be. You can't take more than twice a day.

Ya: Can I also have a bottle of nosedrops?

Pharmacist: Of course Miss.

Ya: How much is this in total?

Pharmacist: One second. The antibiotics, the syrup against coughing and the drops. It is all together 19.83 dollars.

Ya: Please.

Pharmacist: See you. I hope you will get better soon.

（小丫在药店）

药剂师： 下一个是谁？

小丫： 是我。我觉得下一个轮到我了。

药剂师： 小姐，请问你有医生的药方吗？

小丫： 有的，给你。

药剂师： 好了。这些是药片，是抗生素。你每天服用三次，每次两片。记得要在饭前服用。不然的话可能会引起胃部不适。这些药不能与酒精同服。这是糖浆，你每天早晚各喝一茶匙，直到咳嗽好转为止。

小丫： 糖浆就够用了吗？我真的咳得很厉害。

药剂师： 通常情况下这就可以了。每天服用不能超过两次。

小丫： 我能再买一瓶鼻子清洗液吗？

药剂师： 当然可以了，小姐。

小丫： 一共是多少钱？

药剂师： 请稍等。一瓶抗生素、糖浆和鼻子清洗液，一共是19美元83美分。

小丫： 给您。

药剂师： 再见。祝你早日康复。

会话2

Ya: Can you help me? I need to pick out a lotion.

Pharmacist: It would be my pleasure. How can I help you?

Ya: I picked up some poison oak while hiking, and I need something to stop the itchiness.

Pharmacist: We have lotion or cream.

Ya: Which one do you think works better?

Pharmacist: The cream is perhaps longer lasting.

Ya: Is there anything I can take that will help with the itching?

Pharmacist: If you take an antihistamine, that would help a lot.

Ya: Thank you so much for helping me figure out what to do with my poison oak.

Pharmacist: It was a pleasure. Come back anytime.

小丫： 您能帮我吗？我要找一种乳液。

药剂师： 非常荣幸能帮助您。你需要什么呢？

小丫： 我在爬山时被野葛刮伤了，所以我需要些止痒的药。

药剂师： 我们有乳液也有膏状的。

小丫： 哪种更好呢？

药剂师： 膏状的药力更持久。

小丫： 有什么止痒的药吗？

药剂师： 你可以吃一些抗组织胺药片，会有很大帮助。

小丫： 非常感谢帮我想办法。

药剂师： 非常高兴能帮到您。有问题随时来找我。

必备词汇

antibiotics
[ˌæntɪbaɪˈɒtɪks] n.

（用于复数）抗生素

例如 All antibiotics have side effects. 所有抗生素都会产生副作用。

itchy
[ɪtʃi] adj.

发痒的

例如 Wigs are most of the tile itchy and uncomfortable. 假发大多数时候让人感觉发痒，很不舒服。

pill
[pɪl] n.

药丸，药片

pharmacist
[ˈfɑrməsɪst] n.

药剂师

lotion
[ˈloʃən] n.

洗液，护肤液，乳液

例如 To protect and lubricate your skin, apply shaving cream, lotion or gel before shaving. 为了保护和润滑皮肤，可以在剃须前使用一些剃须膏、剃须乳液或者洗涤胶。

pharmacy
['fɑrməsi] n.

药房，药店

例如 Make sure you understand exactly how to take your medicines before you leave the pharmacy. 在离开药房之前，一定要弄明白自己的药该怎么吃。

prescription
[prɪ'skrɪpʃən] n.

药方，处方

例如 Is there anything I can buy without a prescription? 有什么药我无需处方就可以买的？

sufficient
[sə'fɪʃənt] adj.

足够的，充足的

例如 Banks lack sufficient capital to make new loans. 银行缺乏足够的资本来建立新的借贷。

syrup
['sɪrəp] n.

糖浆，糖浆类的药品

例如 cough syrup 止咳糖浆。

地道美语

① **Come back anytime.** 有问题随时回来。是销售人员或营业员对顾客说的话，表示自己随时愿意为顾客服务。例如：

A: This dress is the present for my sister, but I'm not sure if she will fit in.

B: Don't worry. Come back anytime.

A: 这裙子是送给我姐姐的礼物。不知道她能不能穿得下。

B: 别担心。有问题随时回来。

2 **It would be my pleasure、非常荣幸能帮助您。是营业员用语，表示自己非常愿意为对方服务。例如：**

A: Can you please give a brief explanation on the difference between these two products?

B: It would be my pleasure.

A: 你能简单地给我介绍一下这两种产品的区别吗？

B: 非常愿意为您效劳。

3 **Which one do you think works better? 你觉得哪种更有效呢？在购买东西时，顾客常常向销售人员征求意见。例如：**

A: These two models are the best-selling motorcycles.

B: They look totally different. Which one do you think works better?

A: 这两种摩托车型号是我们这儿卖得最好的。

B: 它们看起来完全不同。哪种功效更好呢？

4 **Who is the next? 下一个是谁？在商店里，售货员本着对所有顾客一视同仁的态度，会问下一个顾客是谁。这当然也需要消费者的自觉。**

(In a bakery)

A: Who is the next?

B: I believe it's my turn now. Can I have two white bread please?

（在面包房里）

　A: 下一个是谁？

　B: 我确信轮到我了。我可以要两个白面包吗？

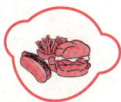

5 Feel free to ask any questions. 有什么问题随时问我。不仅局限于店员和消费者之间，也可以在家人和朋友之间使用。例如：

It was a short explanation. Please feel free to ask if you have any questions.

以上解说很简短。如果有什么问题，请随时问我。

表达方式百宝箱

这节课中出现了在药店买药或者在一般商店中会用到的表达方式，现在就让我们一起来回顾一下吧。

Feel free to ask any questions. 有什么问题随时问我。

It would be my pleasure. 我非常荣幸能帮助您。

Which one do you think works better? 你觉得哪个功效更好？

Who is next? I think it's my turn now. 下一个是谁？我觉得下面轮到我了。

小丫 带你走遍美国

在美国买药

通常，美国医院的医生只负责给病人检查身体，对症开药方。医院里除了供住院病人用药的药房外，没有像国内那种供门诊病人买药的药房，也没有划价一说。病人去医院看完病后，凭医生的处方去药店买药，得了小病可以直接购买非处方药。

美国的药店分为两类：专营药店和药品专柜。专营药店一般门面不大，处方药和非处方药都卖；而药品专柜则往往设在综合性商店或超市的一角。美国和中国药店最大的不同有两点：一是在美国，不论是专营药店还是药品专柜，不论规模大小，都有专业的药剂师给病人提供咨询，而在国内，药店虽然装修华丽，营业员也很多，但具备医学知识的专业人士却很少；二是一些在国内药店可以直接购买的非处方药，在美国却作为处方药，病人必须持有医生的处方才可以买到，像消炎用的抗生素和国内药房里常见的注射剂都属此类。此外，像安定片等神经系统用药在国内药房可以限量购到，但在美国，除美乐通宁（Maletonin）外，所有安眠类药品均属于处方药。

美国法律对药剂师的职责规定很严，也很细，医生的责任和药剂师的责任分得很清楚。医生负责开处方，药剂师则负责管理处方药。作为药剂师，首先要核查药方的真伪和医生是否是执业医师，然后认真判断药量大小是否合适，并可以与医生进一步商量调整用药和改进治疗方案等。之后，药剂师还要将病人所需药品用专门小瓶包装，将病人的姓名、用药方法、每次用量等详细写明，并留下药剂师本人的姓名和电话。最后，药剂师会把处方留下存档，整个过程一般需要1—2个小时。

第31课

去理发店：感受美式服务

情景介绍：理发或美发是日常生活中不可缺少的一部分，尤其对女孩子来说。小丫来到美国后，也要去理发店。下面我们就来看看小丫是怎么应对的吧。

会话1

Ya: I'm ready for a new hairdo. Do you have any suggestions?

Hairdresser: Have you taken a look at any of the new styles lately?

Ya: Yes, I brought a magazine to show you. I would like this one.

Hairdresser: Oh, that is pretty. Do you want to keep your hair this long? Or do you want to take it shorter? I think you would look cute with short hair. Perhaps you should go even shorter than in the picture.

Ya: I'll leave it up to you. Like I said, I'm ready for a change.

Hairdresser: OK. You should really think about getting highlights put in, too.

Ya: Do you think that would look good? I'm worried it will make my hair look unnatural.

Hairdresser: No, it won't. The highlights are very subtle. We can do a little bit this time. If you like it, we can do more next time. Otherwise, the highlights should grow out in about four weeks.

Ya: OK, just do what you want. I count on you. By the way, how much do you charge for a shampoo and set?

Hairdresser: Forty dollars in total.

小丫：我准备换个新发型。你有什么建议吗？

发型师：你有没有留意最近的新发型？

小丫：有。我带了本杂志给你看。我想要这个发型。

发型师：嗯，这个发型很漂亮。你想保留头发现在的长度吗？还是剪短一点。我觉得你短看起来很可爱，你可以考虑剪得比杂志里更短。

小丫：你决定吧。像我说的，我已经准备好要换个形象了。

发型师：好的，你应该考虑把头发外层染成淡一点的颜色。

小丫：你觉得能好看吗？我担心那样会让头发看起来不自然。

发型师：不，不会的，只是稍微染一下。我们可以这次染一点，如果你喜欢，下次再染多一点。如果不喜欢的话，四个星期后颜色就淡下去了。

小丫：好的，那就听你的。顺便问一下，洗头，做头发一共多少钱？

理发师：一共40美元。

必备词汇

hairdo
['hɛr,du] n.

（女子的）发式，发型

例如 a teenager with a punk hairdo 留着朋克发型的少年

hairdresser
['hɛr,drɛsɚ] n.

理发师，美发师。hairdresser's n. 理发店，美发店

例如 If your waitress or a hairdresser looks like that she's having a hard day, leave her an extra tip. 如果为你服务的服务员或理发师看上去日子过得很难，给她一点额外的小费吧。

lately
['letli] adv.

近来，最近，不久前

同义词是recently。

例如 Have you talked to her lately? 你最近有没有和她说过话？

subtle
['sʌtl] adj.

微妙的；敏感的；巧妙的

例如 Subtle changes are taking place every day. 每天都在发生着微妙的变化。

unnatural
[ʌn'næt∫ərəl] adj.

不自然的，违背人性的

例如 He sounds unnatural with the pretending laugh. 假笑让他听起来很不自然。

地道美语

1 I count on you. 我相信你。表示说话者对听话者的完全信任。比I trust you更加口语化。例如：

A: I count on you to choose the best solution for our business.

B: I will try my best.

A: 我相信你能为我们的生意想出最好的办法。

B: 我尽力。

2 I'll leave it up to you. 你决定吧。说话者让听话者来做最后的决定。例如：

A: It's your own choice which university to go to, so I will leave it up to you.

B: I decided to go to Stanford.

    A: 去哪所大学是你自己的选择，所以我让你自己来做决定。

    B: 我决定去斯坦福。

3 Like I said. 像我说过的。指上文已经说过的某句话，为下面要说的话提供指代。例如：

Like I said, this is not the perfect weather to go hiking.

    像我说过的，这样的天气不适合爬山。

4 That is pretty. 那很漂亮。pretty是美式口语中经常出现的一个词，比beautiful使用的频率要高。例如：

She's a very charming and very pretty girl.

    她是一个非常迷人的漂亮女孩。

New York is a very pretty metropolitan.

    纽约是个非常漂亮的大都市。

Life can be pretty complicated.

    生活可以非常复杂。（这里pretty作为副词使用。）

表达方式百宝箱

这节课中小丫在理发店与发型师的对话简单实用，出现了一些征求意见和表达观点的句型。下面就让我们一起来总结一下吧。

I count on you. 我相信你。

I'll leave it up to you. 你决定吧。

Like I said. 像我说的。

That is pretty. 那很漂亮。

小丫 带你走遍 美国

美国著名护肤品牌——倩碧（Clinique）

倩碧（Clinique Laboratories, LLC.）于1968年创立于美国纽约，现隶属于美国雅诗兰黛集团，其推广的基础护肤三步骤世界闻名。

二十世纪60年代后期，人们对肌肤的美丽的概念仅限于一句当时普遍推崇的至理格言——"女性肌肤的状况是与生俱来的，不可改变的"。一位杂志主编提出"女性应该正视她们的肌肤"的言论后，人们才开始发觉，原来肌肤完美可以重塑。这一年是1967年，这位主编就是美国时尚杂志《VOGUE》的主编Carol Philips女士。谁也不曾想到，这位VOGUE杂志的主编日后竟成为化妆品界奇葩——倩碧品牌的创始人之一。她的幸运即来自于她在那篇名为《完美肌肤是否能创造》所提到的独特的护肤理论。该理论一出，震撼人心，也引起Estee Lauder雅诗兰黛家族的注意，不久便聘用Carol创办倩碧化妆品公司，并于1968年在纽约推出。他们在皮肤学专家指道下，通过过敏性测试，成功研制了第一个百分之百不含香料的护肤品牌，那便是Clinique（倩碧）正式创立之日。

就是在1967年，纽约权威的皮肤科专家Dr. Norman Orentreich在接受Carol的专访中表示美丽不是只靠遗传而得的，通过正确的护肤程序，即可改善肌肤状况。女性可以通过主动积极的护肤程序，也就是第一步清洁、第二步清理皮层、第三步滋润的"倩碧护肤三步骤"，让肌肤处于健康自然的完美状态。同时也提出阳光紫外线是伤害肌肤的最大元凶，进而强调防晒的重要性。此理论一出，整个化妆界为之促动。

这篇具有里程碑意义的报道不仅提出精辟的护肤观念，也引起Estee Lauder雅诗兰黛家族的注意，同时也催生了倩碧这一品牌。一切源于偶然，一切又因为偶然而有了契机。这一偶然，不仅创造了倩碧品牌，而且也使倩碧为美容界注入了新的内容与活力。倩碧与爱美女士的一段渊源便有了序曲。

1968年，倩碧这个安全、有效、经由皮肤科专家配方，并且经过过敏性试验、百分之百不含香料的高档化妆品品牌在Estee Lauder公司旗下问世。而为倩碧奠下事业基础的基础护肤三步骤产品：具清洁功效的洗面皂、清理皮层的洁肤水（各类型肌肤均有适合的配方）、和具滋润功效的特效润肤露，就此成为业界的传奇，也成为每个爱美女性不可或缺的护肤产品。

第32课

毕业在即：期待新生活

情景介绍： 时间转瞬即逝，马上就到小丫要毕业的季节了。这几年来在美国的学习和生活让小丫成长了许多，也成熟了许多。面对即将开始的新生活、即将转换的新角色，小丫心里有些疑惑，当然也有很多憧憬。

会话1

Ya: Professor Langman, thank you for the help for the last years. Without your advice and guidance, I wouldn't have been able to complete my studies.

Professor Langman: You are most welcome. It's my duty to give you all the best I can. Of course it's also my honor to have students like you.

Ya: I'm not going to do a master degree for now, but maybe I will change my mind some day in the future. Then I'll definitely want to be your student again.

Professor Langman: I'll be glad to be your teacher again. Even if you are not doing a master degree, you can always ask me questions or just check how I'm doing. After graduation, I'm not your professor any longer, but we can still keep friends.

Ya: I'm so lucky to meet you. We'll keep in touch.

小丫： 朗曼教授，谢谢你这几年来给予我的帮助。没有你的建议和指导，我不可能完成学业。

朗曼教授： 不用客气。为你们提供我的一切是我的责任。当然有你们这样的学生也是我的荣幸。

小丫： 我现在不继续读硕士，但是也许将来的某一天我会改变主意。到时我一定再次做你的学生。

朗曼教授： 我将会非常高兴再次做你的老师。即使你现在不读硕士，你还是可以随时问我问题，或者只是随便问问我过得如何。毕业以后，我就不再

是你的教授了，但是我们依然可以保持朋友的关系。

小丫： 能遇到你我真是太幸运了。我们保持联系。

会话2

Ya: Look at this picture. How naive we were when we were freshmen!

Tom: Yeah, I can't imagine how much people can change in such a short time. We have grown up so much.

Ya: When I think about the days that I just came to the States, there were so many things I didn't know. Thanks to you, I never felt lonely. These four years is the best time of my life, with you, Jerry and Jessica. All of you have taught a lot and gave me a hand without any hesitation when I'm in trouble. I thought I wouldn't have real friends in the States, but I'm so wrong.

Tom: Don't be so sad, we will still see each other after graduation. We all stay in New York. We love this city, and we are not going to leave it. At least not now. Are you planning to attend graduate school?

Ya: Not now. I'm thinking to work for a while first. Get some career experience before I go further with my studies.

Tom: Have you got a job yet?

Ya: Yeah, I've got an assistant designer postion in the APL Advertisement company.

Tom: How is the firm?

Ya: I've finished an internship for 3 months, and I think it's a good firm. It's not really big, but it's got the potential to grow. I have the feeling that I can learn from the firm and I'm willing to grow with it.

Tom: That's very good attitude. Many young people now don't want the hard work. They only want the high wage and long vacation, but they forgot they need to earn it first. Will your family be attending the graduation ceremony?

Ya: Yeah, my parents are coming. I've been in the States for four years, but this is the first time they come here. It's an important moment in my life, so I want them to be here.

Tom: I can understand.

小丫： 看看这张照片，我们大一的时候多幼稚。

汤姆： 是啊，我简直不能想象人在如此短的时间内可以发生这么大的变化。我们都成长了很多。

小丫： 我会想刚来美国的那段日子，有好多东西我都不懂。多亏了有你，我从来没觉得寂寞。这四年是我生命中最美好的一段时光，跟你、杰瑞还有杰西卡一起度过。你们都教给我了很多东西，在我有困难的时候毫不犹豫地伸出援助之手。我原以为在美国不会交到真的朋友，看来我错了。

汤姆： 别这么悲伤。毕业以后我们还是会经常见面的，因为我们都留在纽约。我们爱这座城市，所以我们不想离开它，至少现在不想。你想继续读硕士吗？

小丫： 现在不想。我想先工作一段时间。在我进一步学习之前先积累一些工作经验。

汤姆： 你找到工作了吗？

小丫： 是的，我在APL公司找到了一份助理设计师的工作。

汤姆： 这家公司怎么样？

小丫： 我已经完成了三个月的实习期，我觉得是家好公司。这家公司不是很大，但是它有成长的潜质。我有种感觉我可以从这家公司中学到东西，而且我也愿意和它一起成长。

汤姆： 这是很好的态度。现在许多年轻人不想辛苦工作，只想要高薪水和长假期。但是他们忘记了他们需要先付出。你的家人来参加你的毕业典礼吗？

小丫： 是啊，我父母过来。我来美国有四年了，这还是我父母第一次来。这是我人生中的重要时刻，所以我希望他们在这儿。

汤姆： 我可以理解。

必备词汇

advertisement [əd'və:tismənt, ˌædvə'taizmənt] n.

广告，公告，宣传

commercial advertisement 商业广告；advertisement company 广告公司。

例如 I notice that the advertisement misses out the price of the product. 我注意到广告上不写产品的价格。

freshman
['freʃmən] n.

新手，生手，大学一年级学生

复数形式为freshmen。相应地，大二学生为sophomore，大学三年级学生为junior，大学四年级学生为senior。

例 如 The university provides guidance of all aspects to freshmen students. 这所大学为大一学生提供各方面的指导。

internship
['intə:nʃip] n.

实习生，实习，实习期

internship programs 实习计划；internship report 实习报告。

例 如 We got to know each other at the ad agency where I did an internship for about a month. 我和朋友是在一家广告公司认识的，当时我在这家公司已经实习了差不多一个月。

master degree n.

硕士学位

相应地，学士学位称为bachelor degree；博士学位为doctor degree或者PhD。

例 如 Having a master degree is one of the requirements of this company. 有硕士学历是这家公司招聘的要求之一。

potential
[pəu'tenʃəl] n.

潜能，可能性，潜力

market potential 市场潜力；development potential 发展潜力；potential market 潜在市场。**例 如** He's gifted in music. I think he has the potential of being a great musician. 他有音乐天赋，我觉得他有成为伟大音乐家的潜质。

naive
[nɑːˈiːv] adj.

天真的，纯真的，幼稚的

例如 Freshmen students and new graduates are always very naive. 大学一年级学生跟刚毕业的学生总是很幼稚。

地道美语

1 change my mind 改变主意。这是对客观事实的描述，不带有褒贬色彩。亦可以变换使用其他人称，比如change your mind, change her mind等等，例如：

A: I want to stay home today. I know I said I would go with you yesterday, but I changed my mind.

B: All right then. I'll go alone. Women have the right to change their mind.

A：我今天想待在家。我知道昨天我说会和你一起去，但是我改变主意了。

B：那好吧。我自己去。女人有改变主意的权力。

2 Thanks to you. 多亏了你。这是表示对对方的赞美或者感谢的表达方式。如果对方帮了很大的忙或者由于对方的行为使自己运气好转，便可以使用。例如：

A: I forgot to take the umbrella, but thanks to you, I got home without making myself wet.

B: No problem. It's on the way.

A：我忘了带伞，但是多亏有你，我一点没淋湿就到家了。

B：没问题。正好顺路。

3 Will your family be attending the graduation ceremony? 你的家人会来参加你的毕业典礼吗？句中同时出现了一般将来时和现在进行时，这是美式口语中经常出现的形式，意为"在将来会不会发生某事"。例如：

A: Can I come to your house around 3 o'clock in the afternoon?

B: Of course. Maybe I'll be making the cookies in the kitchen. Just ring the bell, and then I'll come to open the door.

A：我明天下午三点左右可以来你家吗？

B：当然可以了。可能我正在厨房做饼干。到时你只要按门铃就好了，我会马上来给你开门的。

例句中的graduation ceremony意为"毕业典礼"。

---

4 Without your advice and guidance, I wouldn't have been able to complete my studies. 没有你的建议和帮助，我是无法完成学业的。这是对老师或者教授的赞美。这种句式也可以应用在别的情境中。例如：

A: I would have been too late to work without your ride this morning. Thank you so much.

B: It's nothing.

A：今天早晨要不是你送我一程，我就迟到了。真谢谢你。

B：没关系。

5 You are most welcome. 不用客气。这是一种礼貌的表达方式，意思是说"你比谁都受欢迎"，引申为"我最愿意帮助你，千万不要客气之意"。比You are welcome. 的语气更加强烈。例如：

A: Thank you for fixing my car. I wouldn't know how to do it myself.

B: You are most welcome.

A: 谢谢你帮我修好车，我自己都不知道该怎么办。

B: 千万别客气。

表达方式百宝箱

本课中我们的小丫即将结束四年的学习，开始人生的一个新的篇章。对话中，她分别和教授、和汤姆表达了自己对毕业的想法。那么让我们一起来总结和复习一下文中出现的表达方式吧！

change my mind. 改变主意。

Thanks to you. 多亏了你。

Will your family be attending the graduation ceremony? 你的家人会来参加毕业典礼吗？

Without your advice and guidance, I wouldn't have been able to complete my studies. 没有你的建议和指导，我是不能完成学业的。

You are most welcome. 千万不要客气。

小丫 带你走遍美国

美国的毕业典礼

美国一些学校的毕业典礼是在5月，"毕业典礼"的英文表达除了"graduation ceremony"之外，还有一种说法是"commencement"，意为"开始"，取"雄关漫道真如铁，而今迈步从头越"之意。学生踏上征程之前，学校还要请来社会贤达、政坛精英们，为学子们最后一次指点迷津，这是件大事，提前好几个月，由师生共同组成委员会就开始反复搜寻、甄别和邀选讲演者。

有些学校邀请政界或商界名人来为学生们做毕业演讲。到场的名人与学校多少有些因缘。克林顿到宾夕法尼亚大学助兴是因为他的内弟毕业于该校。2000年哥伦比亚大学请到了当朝副总统、民主党总统候选人戈尔。戈尔的一个女儿在哥伦比亚大学法学院毕业，做父亲的到场祝贺、祝福是好事成双。典礼这天，毕业生都是一身蓝色的学袍。蓝色是哥伦比亚大学的标色，袖口的三杠是博士，两杠是硕士，一杠是学士。戈尔是黑袍红领。这是他母校的标色（美国八所常青藤母校都有自己的标色）。学袍可以算是衣钵中的衣，所以讲演者和教授都披着各自母校的校袍。

在每年的毕业典礼上，哈佛大学校长会对成绩A类的学生说：恭喜你们，以最优异的成绩从哈佛大学毕业，相信10年以后诺贝尔奖的获得者将从你们中间诞生；对成绩B类的学生说：恭喜你们，以优秀的成绩从哈佛大学毕业，相信10年以后为哈佛大学捐资助学的人将从你们中间诞生；对成绩C类的学生说：恭喜你们，以合格的成绩从哈佛大学毕业，相信10年以后你们将成为各行各业中的佼佼者。

在毕业典礼上，大学权杖（University Mace）是最先入场的。权杖是学校的象征，起源于中世纪，进场时全场起立行注目礼。号旗（gonfalon）与之类似，每个学院有各自不同的号旗，代表一个权力单位。毕业典礼上，毕业生代表，即号旗手，手持各学院的号旗入场。

小丫怀着远大的梦想只身一人来到大洋彼岸的美国求学，在这里她学到了知识，结识了一些此生难忘的朋友，也学会了一种不同的生活方式，并从中成长成熟了起来。我们都见证了小丫的成长之路，希望小丫在新的角色中会更加出色。